THE BONHOEFFERS

PORTRAIT OF A FAMILY

THE
BONHOEFFERS

PORTRAIT OF A FAMILY

Sabine Leibholz-Bonhoeffer

SIDGWICK & JACKSON
London

Originally published by Johannes Kiefel Verlag,
Wuppertal-Barmen, Germany, 1968
First published in U.K. by Sidgwick & Jackson Ltd,
1971
Copyright © by Sabine Leibholz-Bonhoeffer

ISBN 0 283 97811 2

Printed in Great Britain by
Willmer Brothers Limited, Birkenhead
for
Sidgwick and Jackson Limited
1, Tavistock Chambers, Bloomsbury Way,
London W.C.1

To Eugen Rosenstock-Huessy on his 80th birthday

Foreword

No German name of this century is more honoured than that of Dietrich Bonhoeffer. He stands out unassailed and unassailably, his reputation growing with each decade, par excellence the model of a good and indeed a great German. Although he was not quite 40 when he was executed by the Nazis, his written works, including the famous *Letters from Prison*, have profoundly affected theology here and elsewhere alike on the technical and popular levels.

But if he had never written a line for publication, the story of his last years, his undeviating opposition to Hitler, his return at the outbreak of war from a safe haven in America, his active participation in the resistance, his sublime end would have left a stirring legend.

As we study his life, we appreciate without effort the complete integration between his theology and his heroism, and the burning faith which inspired them both. But having said so much, we have hardly begun to depict the full man who emerges from the definitive biography by Eberhard Bethge, and from the story of his family told here by his twin sister, to which Dr Bethge has contributed a valuable preface.

Theologians are not always lovable or attractive nor, for that matter, are heroes. But Dietrich Bonhoeffer throughout his short life won everyone's heart, beginning with his large and brilliant family and notably including Dr Bell, Bishop of Chichester, who appears here as in other books about Germany as an incomparable Christian.

From many letters quoted and countless small touches, fresh light is thrown here on the secret of his personal potency. The book can fairly be called indispensable reading for the multitude already interested in him in a score of countries.

But this is not just another excellent book about Dietrich Bonhoeffer, though that alone would give it a host of readers. It is the story of the Bonhoeffer family, and surely no family of our time, even including the Kennedys, has been more remarkable than the Bonhoeffers, with their distinguished ancestry on both sides, their father perhaps the leading psychiatrist in Germany, the eight children all extremely gifted. And when the supreme crisis came, two sons and two sons-in-law laid down their lives in the struggle against the Nazis.

At the end, their father could write with quiet justice: 'We are sad, but also proud of their attitude which has been consistent. We have fine memories of both sons from prison, which are deeply touching to both of us and their friends.' (Quoted from Dr Bethge's Biography.)

Just previously came the significant words: 'We were all agreed on the need to act'. The collective force of the family ethic inspired from start to finish all the Bonhoeffers, including the present authoress.

Dr Bethge brings out effectively the double theme of her book— the martyrdom of one twin and the exile of the other. It is not difficult to detect similar ideals of duty at work on the plane of high tragedy in Germany and of discomfort, neglect and loneliness (along with much kindness) in England. As one reads Frau Leibholz's reaction to her honoured husband's internment for a while, one realizes that alike in brother and sister the sense of dedication was total. Her comments on the British character from a number of unusual vantage points are fair, penetrating and humorous. This passage makes delightful reading, though it cannot have been a delightful experience: 'The women refugees, many of whom came of good families, frequently had to take posts as domestic servants in English familes. Even though they were highly prized for the excellence of their work, they were still not accorded the consideration which was their due. Occasionally they were actually given different names, for instance, the name of the last cook employed at the house concerned. In other words, their employers had not sometimes accustomed themselves to the new name.'

Basically she admires the English for the most agreeable of possible reasons—their intrinsic fair play and decency, and expresses deep gratitude to a number of English men and English women.

Her return to Germany 'in the early summer of 1947' has a special poignancy for myself. I also, in the early summer of 1947, was paying a first visit to Germany since pre-war days. I descended from my aeroplane as Minister for the British Zone of Germany, an area at that time with no government of its own, no real money and singularly little fuel or food. I proclaimed my immediate confidence in a spiritual and material recovery to come, and so it is clear did she, implicitly, as her book ends as she went back home. She was testifying out of the profound knowledge of her people, in spite of her years of absence, I from nothing but Christian optimism. But Christian optimism has not in fact proved a bad guide to what has since been accomplished in Germany.

One could hardly expect to find many Bonhoeffers available, but one could expect, and one did find countless Germans, high and low, who carried within themselves some small portion of the Bonhoeffer spirit.

LORD LONGFORD

Contents

Illustrations

Preface

There are two focal points to this book: a German family and its exile in England during the period of National Socialism. Dietrich Bonhoeffer has become a symbol of Christian resistance far beyond the borders of Germany. Now his twin sister tells us the story of her family background and circle. This means, however, that it will be concerned with the life of what was, in the best sense of the phrase, a family of leading citizens. Thus it was a lively sense of responsibility towards mankind that led to the sacrifice of four of its menfolk, not only Dietrich himself but Klaus Bonhoeffer and the two brothers-in-law, Hans von Dohnanyi and Rüdiger Schleicher, as well. What the author is describing, then, is the exile which she and her circle had to live through in England while the events leading up to that fateful climax were maturing and coming to fruition in the homeland.

A strong tension is apparent throughout in the way in which these two areas of human experience were related to one another. The awareness of what life was like in the one made the experience of living in the other almost unendurably painful. Yet at the same time fresh depths of experience were being gained in either sphere from the fact of what was being endured in the other. Today both are in danger of falling into oblivion.

Nowadays it is rare to come across such families, with their deep inner resources and the harmony between their members. Yet it is no nostalgic romanticism that prompts us to look into a family history of this kind, with its maturity, its experience of suffering and also the wisdom of the early training by which it has been guided (there is in any case so much of the past that can never be repeated even in such a story as this). On the contrary the spirit in which we view this narrative is full of meaning for the future, for we recognize it as an element in that history of the German spirit which is indispensable if a new generation is to discover its own identity.

And the exile? Our vision of the world belonging to this is today becoming dangerously blurred. Surely it can be no accident that while the great lexicons of theology and of the Church do, for instance, include detailed articles on the expellees from the East, they tell us nothing about what the exile meant as this took shape over the thirty years. In the year 1939—at this time I was still remote from the Bonhoeffers but was an admirer of the unity and strength of this family—I had a meeting with Sabine Leibholz, née Bonhoeffer, and her husband in London when their exile had just begun. In my naïveté and optimism I regarded this sojourn abroad as no more than an interlude, though in truth, far from being a voluntary 'exodus', it was an expulsion. It seemed to me that it was an unavoidable, but still tolerable, way of 'passing the winter', and that England was an enviable refuge. I thought, so to say, that the wheel would turn again for them, and that they would once more return to take up what they had just laid down. At that stage I never realized that a truer image was that of an irreversible process of history, at once demanding and enriching, which day by day left its mark upon the faces and the spirits of those drawn into it.

In the year 1946—in the meantime I had myself come, through marriage, to belong to the family circle—I was able to visit Sabine and her family as a first emissary from Berlin to Oxford. The joy of seeing her again was mingled with pain at the terrible sufferings of the Bonhoeffers in Berlin. Nevertheless Oxford still continued to seem to me an 'enviable refuge'. We believed that it was we at home who had had the really important experiences. The insatiable questions of those at Oxford about every detail, great or small, seemed only to confirm still further the idea that the exile was a mere temporary episode. It was only years later—probably beginning with that moment in 1947 when the exiles returned to Berlin—that it gradually dawned upon me how wrong it had been to think of the exile as a mere episode, and what far-reaching changes the events belonging to it had in reality brought about on both sides.

In Berlin, too, there could be no simple resumption of old ties and old ways of life. The ordeals which had been endured, mounting to an inconceivable climax (nights of bombing, the race to overthrow the régime before being arrested and imprisoned, and finally the total collapse) had made that impossible. Yet at the same time these ordeals did contain one sustaining element: a direct awareness of the 'whither' and the 'wherefore' of it all. Even the prison cell and death itself were endured amid the circle who shared a common mind and, in the broadest sense of the term, a common language. In Oxford, for want of an exchange of news, such a meagre information as was gleaned about what was taking place in the homeland secretly and beneath the surface had perforce to remain shadowy and indirect.

Certainly those concerned identified themselves completely with the interests of the family in Berlin as well as with those of the host country. But there still remained as factors in the situation the delicacy of their position as aliens in the English scene and the embarrassing silence they had to maintain on what was going on in Germany. Whereas for those at home disaster, even in its most violent and painful forms, made its impact in the broader context of common life and activity: those in exile were exposed to a twofold isolation and condemned to the passive role of remaining constantly and painfully on the *qui vive*. Over and above this there was the lack of sympathy and understanding which they sometimes had to experience. This might be due to a certain naïveté on the part of those who had never known any other home except England, or to the way in which the authorities carried out their instructions. But it might also take the form of a well-meant readiness to offer help.

If the émigrés survived this threat to their personalities, then they must have gained something which we in Germany must not lose. If we are found wanting in our readiness to accept them, then this can only have the effect of isolating the émigrés afresh. But this will be at our people's peril. It is already perilous that in the field of politics a party leader of our own day can actually believe it possible to make capital from the fact that his opponent in the other party was an 'émigré'. Yet in Goethe himself we can read: 'Thus should the German people hold firm to their attitude ... receiving the world and contributing to it ...; but not sinking into the stupid obstinacy of a tasteless self-regard and self-glorification.... Unhappy people! ... For the best of them have always lived in exile'. Again, immediately after the war Thomas Mann spoke of a 'yawning abyss which divides our experiences from the experiences of those who remained behind in Germany'. Indeed at that time he actually believed himself forced to conclude: 'It is quite impossible to bridge this abyss and get beyond it, so as to arrive at a common understanding'.

Thomas Mann must not be proved right. Only very few of those who shared in the exile are still alive today. But however small the number may be, the knowledge of what they endured and of what they contributed at such great cost to themselves must not be suppressed. Unless we duly recognize the significance of all that they were and all that they achieved we shall never ourselves gain any firm identity of our own. Our attitude towards them acquires the force of a sure and irrefutable sign of our own condition.

The story of a private family life recorded in these pages has, by the sheer fact of being so well told, been raised to a plane where it can spread its influence far and wide. Its special significance and its importance for society as a whole consist, first, in the fact that it makes it far more difficult to forget the abyss— not only that spoken of by Thomas Mann but also that which divides the nations—and, second, that it contributes towards the bridging of this twofold abyss.

EBERHARD BETHGE
Rengsdorf, August 1968

PART ONE

FAMILY LIFE

1

My Parents

Once one has celebrated one's sixtieth birthday, and parents, friends, and five brothers and sisters have already died, an insistent desire arises in one to give permanent form to one's pictures of them. It was this that prompted me to undertake sketches of the lives of my seven brothers and sisters and a portrait of my parents. I also wanted to set down certain personal experiences from the years which we spent in England as refugees from Hitler's Germany. I must confess that some reservations did occur to me. But since these experiences are representative of a fate which befell millions of innocent individuals in similar, albeit in much harsher, forms, and which brought death to them, they must not be passed over in silence here, any more than the fate which befell my brothers and sisters when they set themselves to resist the crimes of the National Socialist régime, regarding it as worth the cost to lay down their lives on behalf of freedom, human dignity, justice, and truth.

Yet before we come to mourn our dead, light must be cast upon those times in which a different order prevailed, an order which seemed to us then firmly established enough to last for ever, an order imbued with Christian meaning, in which we could pass a sheltered and secure childhood.

On the 1st September 1939 Hitler's troops invaded Poland, and on Sunday the 3rd September 1939 Chamberlain made the following announcement transmitted throughout the British broadcasting system: 'Great Britain finds herself in a state of war with Germany. She stands by her treaty with Poland'. At that time my

husband, our daughters and I were in Hastings, as refugees from
Hitler, and we heard the announcement while gathered round the
radio among English people. Our youngest daughter, Christiane,
was exactly the same age as I had been when the First World
War began in 1914.

At its outbreak twenty-five years earlier I was a child of eight.
At that time we smaller members of the family were at our holiday home in Friedrichsbrunn in the Harz Mountains, and for me
that momentous August day of 1914 is primarily associated with
the memory of how at that very moment the village was celebrating its local shooting festival. Our governess suddenly dragged
us away from the pretty, enticing market stalls and the merry-go-
round which was being pulled by a poor white horse, so as to
bring us back as quickly as possible to our parents in Berlin.
Sadly I looked at the now emptying scene of the festivities, where
the stall-holders were hastily pulling down their tents. In the late
evening we could hear through the window the songs and shouts
of the soldiers in their farewell celebrations. Next day, after the
adults had hastily done the packing, we found ourselves sitting
in the train to Berlin.

My father was forty-six at the time, and therefore already
beyond the age of conscription. He now became a specialist
consultant on psychiatry and neurology to the Corps of Guards,
but remained in his post at the Charité Clinic. He also continued
his work as a university professor. During the war years my
mother was very much occupied, although certainly she always
had good and faithful servants. Very bitter losses were soon being
suffered by our wider circle of relations, and my mother felt these
with all her heart, while for our father, too, the very first months
of the war in 1914 brought much sorrow. We were told that
three of our cousins had fallen in the West, that our cousin
Lothar Bonhoeffer had had his leg crushed and an eye shot out,
and that another cousin had had to have his leg amputated.
A lasting impression was made upon me by my wounded cousin
Lothar, half blinded and limping on crutches, head and leg swathed
in bandages, yet quite unbroken in spirit and still continuing to
sing his soldier songs and songs by Hermann Löns. Also I can
still vividly picture today my gentle, fair-haired, blue-eyed and
slender seventeen-year-old cousin Hans von der Goltz, who had
joined the Elisabethers. Even though he was wearing his blue

4

uniform when he made his farewell visit he still did not look in the least like a warrior. Very soon he, too, had fallen.

My parents' first home in Berlin was situated near the Tiergarten, with windows looking out on the Bellevue Park. Our governess, a monarchist heart and soul, took a great interest in the Kaiser's children who could be seen playing there. Sometimes on our walks in the Tiergarten she heard the hooting—'tatutata—just like papa', as the Berliners used to say, and then she would run with us to the Charlottenburg Chaussee, where Kaiser Wilhelm II or the crown prince were driving by in their cars. When we reported these adventures at home we were laughed at.

Soon after the initial battles of 1914 in East Prussia my mother took in her old nanny who had fled from Königsberg together with her daughter. The daughter, who went for walks with us little ones, was understandably interested in the 'nailing' of the 'iron Hindenburg', a huge wooden figure which had been set up. In return for fifty pfennig one was given a broad round-headed nail which had to be nailed into his sleeve. The best nail of all was a gold one which could be had for five marks, the money going, if my memory is correct, to the Red Cross.

On one occasion Fräulein Lenchen bought me a little brooch with 'now we'll thrash them' written on it. I was very proud to have it glittering on my white collar, but at midday when I showed myself to my parents with it on my father said, 'Hallo, what have you got there? just give it to me,' and it disappeared into his pocket. 'Where did you get that?' asked Mama, and both my parents promised me a prettier brooch which Mama would look out for me.

My mother was a very intelligent woman. My husband expressed his opinion that this fact struck one anew every time one had a conversation with her. She was full of courage and optimism. Her speech was natural and vivacious. It was a matter of indifference to her what others thought of her, she did what she considered right. She took the problems of others very much to heart, was always ready to help, and was loved and honoured by many who crossed her path and had occasion to experience her warmth and generosity.

Her father, an amiable and moderate man, son of Karl von Hase, the Church historian, was court chaplain to the Potsdam

Garrison Church. He was a much-travelled man and this had
enabled him to pursue his interests in theology, history and the
visual arts. But the career of a military chaplain held little interest
for him. From 1871 onwards he was in continuous contact with
the future Kaiser Friedrich. His tenure of office as court chaplain
under Wilhelm II ended with a disappointment, with the result
that he went to Breslau as professor of theology. Here my
mother grew up in a circle of intellectually alert and interesting
figures. She was self-confident and an excellent hostess. It was
probably from her mother, Clara, née the Countess Kalckreuth,
that she inherited her artistic bent, her good taste, the pleasure
she took in singing, and her talent for painting. She had heard
many songs from her mother, who had also been a pupil of Clara
Schumann (wife of the composer, Robert Schumann) and of
Liszt. While still a young girl my mother was greatly interested
in education. At a time when most of the girls with whom she
came into contact regarded themselves as amply fulfilled by
domestic and social duties, she decided to take the teachers'
examination. My father set down his first impression of her in the
following terms: 'In the winter of 1896 I attended an open
evening at the house of the physicist, Oscar Meyer. There I met
a young, fair, blue-eyed girl whose bearing was so free and
natural, and whose expression was so open and confident, that
as soon as she entered the room she took me captive. This
moment when I first laid eyes upon my future wife remains in
my memory with an almost mystical force.' Our mother gave
us eight children a wonderful childhood. She had great peda-
gogic talents and was always consistent in her treatment of us
but never 'schoolmistressy'. She taught all of us herself at home
for a few years and only then did we have to go to school. 'No'
remained 'no', but she much preferred to say 'yes' whenever
it was at all possible. Nobody understood better how to bring us
round to her point of view or how to help solve our problems,
and she had an ever-resourceful imagination for entering into
our games. It would have been impossible to answer her back
impertinently, and if we were disrespectful to others she did not
hesitate to box our ears. All through our childhood she took part
in our prayers and sang our evening hymns with us. The first
time I saw my mother cry was when Dietrich, aged nine,
broke one of his front teeth during physical training and had

to be given an artificial one. I did not find that so terrible and was quite dismayed at Mama's tears.

When we were sick a degree of care was devoted to us such as is rarely seen today. At such times our family doctor, Dr Senz, who always smelt faintly of eau-de-cologne, used to accompany Mama to the sickroom. Before examining us he would rub his hands together energetically, but they still never failed to give us a cold shudder. After any illness two days in bed without fever was the rule. Bed linen and night shirts were changed again and again. Great care was taken in deciding our diet. The rooms were tidied and aired with special thoroughness. If we could not have baths we were made to lie on several towels and were soaped all over from head to foot. If we spent a bad night or broke out in a sweat, someone in charge would bring fresh linen and rub us with French spirits. If we had to lie quiet, books were read to us and we could choose which we wanted. We liked this especially. On the other hand, my mother did not make much fuss. For instance on one occasion when I was two I refused to eat. But when the nursemaid anxiously sought my mother's advice Mama decided: 'We will let her go without until she is ready to eat again, and, what is more, to eat the same food'. And she was right. Next day I ate with a good appetite.

Even in her old age Mama had an infallible memory for poetry and she bequeathed something of this to me, a gift which still helps me through many a sleepless hour. There was no place for false piety or any kind of bogus religiosity in our home. Mama expected us to show great resolution. For instance when she saw my brother Klaus hesitating on the springboard she simply jumped in, even though she herself could not swim.

Our parents created a second home for us at Friedrichsbrunn in the eastern Harz Mountains which could be reached quickly from Berlin. Some of our happiest childhood memories are of the holidays we spent there. The journey, in two specially reserved compartments under the supervision of Fräulein Horn, was a joy in itself. At Thale two carriages and pairs would already be waiting for us, one for the smallest members of the party and the adults and one for the luggage. Most of the heavy luggage would have been sent on ahead and two housemaids would have travelled on in advance a few days earlier to clean and warm the house. At other times the house was looked after by Frau

Sanderhoff, who lived with her family in a small cottage nearby in the grounds. She, too, would help in the maids' preparations, having previously made sure that we had firewood and vegetables, and her husband would have mown the meadows where we liked to romp.

From Thale we still had six kilometres further to travel to Friedrichsbrunn. The boys always made the journey on foot, for it was a beautiful route through leafy forests and on higher ground through fir-trees interspersed with fine vistas. It was always a very special occasion when our parents came to visit us and two of us were then allowed to travel down to Thale with the carriage to bring them back. When the road became steep my father used to jump out of the carriage and walk up beside the coachman and the horses.

In the meantime, at Friedrichsbrunn, we would have lit up the house with little cup candles which we used to place in all the windows. Thus even from afar the house would be aglow to greet the new arrivals. On walks with our parents, Mama would be most entertaining, and often when the path became steep my father would warn her not to talk too much to us. He also never allowed us to hang onto her or 'give' our nosegays to her when we found it a bore to carry them ourselves.

There was a special stand used for shooting contests at the local shooting festival, which we only approached with great awe. It had a specially constructed pit for the scorer which was two metres deep, and one of the village children of three years old had fallen into it and been drowned when it had become filled with rain water. This was the first time that we heard, with grief and shock, of a child of our own personal acquaintance dying. I can still vividly remember that after the hole had been pumped out and covered over the adults quoted the saying, 'the well is covered when the child has already fallen in', and Dietrich and I made it the subject of our nine-year-old philosophisings.

Among my first impressions there stands in my memory another event which took place during one of our happy holidays at Friedrichsbrunn, and which frightened us very much. It was a hot July day when our governess, Fräulein Horn, accompanied us three little ones and my sister Ursula to the mountain lake where we used to swim. As we made our way there through the heat Fräulein Horn warned us, 'Children, wait a little before

going into the water. Cool off a bit first!' After we had put on
our bathing costumes, therefore, we sat down obediently by the
lake and waited until Fräulein Horn allowed us to go in. But our
kindergarten teacher, Fräulein Lenchen, ran straight into the
water and, with a series of swift strokes, had already reached the
centre of the lake when she suddenly sank. Dietrich was the first
to notice it and uttered a piercing cry. At one glance Fräulein
Horn took in what had happened. I can still see her throw her
watch-chain aside and, in her long woollen skirt, swim out with
strong, swift strokes, shouting back to us over her shoulder, 'Stay
on the shore everyone!'

We were seven years old and could not yet swim. We cried
and trembled and held on very firmly to little Susie. We could
hear our dear Fräulein Horn crying out to the drowning woman,
'Keep swimming! Keep swimming!'. We saw how difficult it was
for Fräulein Horn to save Lenchen and bring her back. At first
Lenchen hung onto her neck, but soon became unconscious,
and we heard Fräulein Horn exclaiming 'Help me dear God,
help me!' as she swam back with Fräulein Lenchen on her back.
Fräulein Lenchen, still unconscious, was laid down on her side.
Fräulein Horn put her finger down her throat so as to let out the
water. Dietrich gently patted her on the back and we all crouched
round Fräulein Lenchen. Soon she recovered consciousness and
Fräulein Horn said a long prayer of thanksgiving. Afterwards
there was still an hour's walk home through the beautiful beech
forest. Fräulein Horn's ankle-length woollen skirt was dripping
wet and slapped against her legs, and afterwards she became ill.
During the nineteen years that she lived with us, right up to the
time of her marriage, this was her only illness.

In 1916, when the shortage of food in Berlin was becoming
more and more acute, we set up home in a large house with a
pretty garden in the Grunewald at 14 Wangenheimstrasse. There
we were able to keep goats and poultry and in this way improve
our food supply to some extent. In my mother's opinion our
big brothers, who were growing fast and would perhaps very
soon be called up, needed plenty to eat. It was one of her most
anxious cares to make sure that they had this. She knew what
hunger meant. One day in 1918, when it was feared that the
'Spartakist' groups in the western suburbs were going to invade
the district, my mother gave the following instructions to our

cook: 'Above all, Anna, prepare plenty of good coffee for them and a lot of cakes!'. In fact, however, everything remained quiet in the Grunewald. Again, on one occasion an intruder had crept into the house by way of a tree onto the balcony upstairs and had hidden himself under a sofa. But while my brothers held him fast and deprived him of his lock-picking tool the first thing that she asked him was whether he was hungry and would like something to eat!

Our mother had a particular gift for celebrating special occasions. Together with our father she used to give us the prettiest dances and fancy-dress balls. She was herself quite good at acting and we children, too, performed many plays at home. There was a large 'costume' chest with all kinds of costumes and wigs. When Mama read aloud the very simplicity of her way of speaking had a particularly moving quality of its own. So, too, with her singing. Dietrich always accompanied her. As soon as she started singing the door would softly open and my father would enter on tiptoe and sit down in the background. This was still the time when the needs of the large household were looked after by five servants. Only the organization was my mother's responsibility, and thus she remained free to look after the essentials, namely our father and her sons and daughters.

How hard it must have been for our parents during the inflation in 1922–3 when everyone's money melted away! At that time all earnings had to be changed straightaway into food and things for the household because next week the devaluation would advance even more rapidly. Our carpenter lamented to my mother, 'Madam, you are the only one who pays the bill straightaway. All the others wait and wait.' If anyone spoke of our parents as 'rich people' my mother always made the rejoinder, 'Oh, yes, rich in children!' or 'There are so many to divide between!'

Within the space of seven years there were six marriages in our family, and between 1923 and 1929 my kind mother provided all the furniture and household requirements for the new homes of her four daughters, as is usual in Germany. It gave her pleasure but at the same time it was a very great strain to undertake these constant journeys into the city where it was most difficult to obtain many things immediately after the inflation. The plans she so lovingly made on our behalf and her perseverance in carrying them out were touching. On every shopping expedition she would allow herself a brief respite from her cares with a cup of coffee and a cake or a little clear soup and a small pasty, and then, freed from her household problems, she would give herself to her companion in the most congenial way, ready for conversation on any topic. This would continue until, with the words, 'Well, I must gather myself together', she would pay the bill, leave a very generous tip and hurry away. On one occasion she said to us girls, 'Probably we believe that at sixteen we understand our mothers, but we only really understand our mothers when we have children of our own'.

Our father was born on the 31st March 1868. His ancestors had been settled at Schwäbisch Hall since 1513, and many of them have honoured graves there in the Michaeliskirche. Their earlier forebears had been goldsmiths, aldermen and theologians while the more recent ones were doctors and lawyers. In 1912, our father had been appointed to the chair of neurology and psychiatry at the university of Berlin, and had taken over the university clinic for nervous and psychiatric disorders.

Probably what struck one most about our father were his expressive eyes and the very mobile face which he kept completely under control. He had a well-formed head and dark hair. His limbs were graceful and his movements very elastic. His hands, too, were remarkable and full of expression. His gestures were extremely gentle and controlled. By nature our father was somewhat remote and reserved, and yet when he looked at anyone his eyes were full of intense understanding. If he wanted to emphasize some point he did so by intonation and never by raising his voice. Professor Scheller has said of him: 'Just as he utterly disliked all that is immoderate, exaggerated or undisciplined, so too, in his own person everything was completely controlled.'

He taught us by his example, by the manner and form in which he conducted his daily life. He spoke little and his judgements were conveyed to us by a raised eyebrow, a joke or occasionally even a gently ironic smile. He had an extraordinarily clear eye for the genuine, the spontaneous, the creative. He let us feel how much he respected warm-hearted, selfless and self-controlled behaviour, and trusted us to stand by the weaker party. Above all, he hoped that we would truly learn to distinguish the essential from the inessential, and would come to recognize our own limitations. His great tolerance left no room for narrow-mindedness and broadened the horizons of our home. He took it for granted that we would try to do what was right and expected much from us, but we could always count on his kindness and the fairness of his judgement. He had a great sense of humour and often helped us to overcome inhibitions with a timely joke. He had too firm a grip upon his own emotions to allow himself ever to speak a word to us which was not wholly suitable. His dislike of clichés did at times make some of us inarticulate and uncertain of ourselves. But it had the effect that as adults we no longer had any taste for catchwords, gossip, commonplaces or loquacity. He, himself, would never have used a catchword or a 'trendy' phrase.

In all that pertained to our education our parents stood united as a wall. There was not question of one saying one thing and the other something else. My father's exclamation of reproach, 'Pfui', could be inimitable in its effectiveness. It is true that this was rarely used, and chiefly on those occasions on which one of us did not show sufficient self-control when he had hurt himself or did not quickly pick himself up again when he had fallen or when he exaggerated his pain in order to draw attention to himself and to gain sympathy. At the same time our father was the most loving and careful binder-up of wounds. On one occasion when it became necessary for him to give us a quick injection, our family doctor not being available, it was obvious that he would much rather have given the injection to himself. It was very much frowned upon if someone forgot to carry out a commission received from our grandmother, for instance to bring her something back from the city. We were even then made to realize that such forgetfulness in the young was egoism and inexcusable thoughtlessness, whereas if my mother forgot something it was because it was too much to demand and because she lacked the strength.

Our father was probably the ultimate authority which we recognized. If our mother said, 'Papa would not like that', this was enough to ensure that it would not happen. When our father entered the room it would have been impossible to ignore it. He was a master of making the best use of his time. Without ever having recourse to the excuse of 'I haven't the time', he managed to achieve an incredible amount in the course of his day without pressing himself unduly. 'Don't rush, Pauline', he often used to exclaim to my mother.

Our family home was a focal point and a meeting place for the wider circle of our relations, and—something that does not follow automatically—was able to attract the sons- and daughters-in-law as well, and not only on festive occasions but in times of trouble too, for our parents made our problems their own. If there were tears in the eyes of her grown-up children then my mother's eyes, too, would immediately fill with tears, though she did not cry at all easily on her own account. My parents were hardly ever separated. Each was only 'half a person' without the other. In a marriage lasting fifty years they managed to restrict their times of separation to a few weeks.

2

Schooldays

When I was ten years old, I was sent to the school of Fräulein Adelheid Mommsen, a daughter of Theodor Mommsen the famous historian. The children who went there were from homes and families known to Fräulein Mommsen. She was extremely proficient, puritanical, and cosmopolitan in her outlook. She had taken two little girls who were orphans and half Greek by nationality into her house, cared for them with devotion, and later adopted them and given them an education. The school was furnished in a spartan manner. It was only much later and in England that I again found schools with this predilection for the greatest possible simplicity.

The school was housed in a garden flat and the garden behind served as the playground during breaks. The school was divided into four classes only, and Fräulein Mommsen herself, together with her assistant teachers, few in number but excellent, were responsible for the tuition. The classes were small, consisting of between eight and fifteen pupils. The summer holidays were long, almost three months, and on one day in every week there was no school. Initially my elder sisters had begun their education at a school in the city, but my mother was not pleased with the tone there, and so they had already become pupils at Fräulein Mommsen's when I entered the school.

One of the members of my class was Vera von Trott zu Solz, a daughter of the then Minister of Education, and at her house I also met Adam von Trott, who was later associated with my brothers in the resistance to Hitler and who was executed after the 20th July.

When we sang our morning hymn at school Vera was the most whole-hearted in joining in. The sandwiches she brought to eat during break—a matter of interest to us children in those hungry years—were the most meagre in our class. When I was invited to lunch with the Trotts—I believe there were already six little Trotts gathered round the table—the food we ate had been fetched from the public wartime kitchens. Once, as the Trotts were playing with us in the garden, Dietrich said to me, 'I do think Vera is nice'. Unfortunately they soon departed when their father retired from office to live on their estate at Imshausen.

In 1917, Fräulein Mommsen accepted a girl of English-Jewish descent as one of her pupils. She was put into our class. With her long stiff curls and her precocious self-assurance she cut a rather alien figure among us. I soon noticed that some of my classmates wanted to put her in coventry. This made me indignant and I befriended her. My former friends tried to draw me away, but at that time I already thought such conduct very unkind, and after some time I succeeded in bridging the gap between them and this child. The little girl was accepted.

In 1918, Fräulein Mommsen accepted two Jewish sisters from Erlangen and put them in my class, which, including them, numbered only seven pupils. They did not take part in religious instruction, and I believe that this made their position difficult. Straightaway two mothers complained about the 'affront' involved in including the two little Jewish girls. But Fräulein Mommsen remained firm and would not allow their views to sway her. Some of my fellow pupils, too, made it clear to the little girls that they wanted to have nothing to do with them. By contrast, Vera von Trott was particularly nice to them, and I, too, made friends with them. The younger of the two, who was thirteen, was extremely gifted and mentally alert, far more so than I was. She had already read Thomas Mann, Keller's *Grüne Heinrich* and C. F. Meyer's *Jürg Jenatsch*, books which I had not yet read at that time, though under her influence I soon began to do so. The sisters were inseparable and very reserved. I was never able to reach the point where these two little girls would visit me at home. It was clear that their parents wanted them to confine their social contacts to Jewish homes only. In 1920, some girls made so bold as to come to school with little silver swastikas round their necks. Fräulein Mommsen forbade them to wear these swastikas in the school.

Since we were a family of eight lively brothers and sisters, the friendships we made at school did not play a very important part in our lives. The children of the neighbourhood were more important to us, and for us younger ones it was our elder brothers who in many respects provided our standards and set the tone for us. All eight of us were very different from one another in temperament, gifts and interests, as also in our looks. And yet there was something that united us, something that we owed to our parents. I hope that in attempting to provide these character-sketches I shall be able to make this apparent.

3

Karl-Friedrich

Born on the 13th January 1899, Karl-Friedrich was the eldest son, seven years older than I. My mother used to say that if he had not come at the head of the list none of us would have come to any good. It was plain that soon he was as reliable as a nurse-maid. His selflessness was striking. Invariably he took the smallest portion of food, and this trait lasted throughout his life. He was always top of his form without doing much work. He seemed to have plenty of free time, and enjoyed painting and going to museums.

At fourteen he worked out with great accuracy the family tree of the Bonhoeffers, tracing it back to the fifteenth century, and he painted this family tree upon a broad sheet of canvas. Thenceforward it hung in the well of the stairs until it was destroyed by the bombing in 1945. As a boy, Karl-Friedrich did much painting but soon became captivated by physics, an interest which remained with him for the rest of his life. In 1918 when he went to serve in the army he took his physics books with him in his knapsack. He was not in the least interested in sport, but he often made expeditions lasting many hours through the woods, and greatly enjoyed these.

The death of our brother Walter, who fell in April 1918, was a terrible blow to him. Karl-Friedrich himself was also wounded, and when he returned from the trenches in 1918 he had become a socialist. Despite this, he retained a strong sense of tradition. He was full of admiration for the manifold gifts, including artistic ones, which he had discovered among the simple soldiers, gifts which, as he then believed, had never been brought to light because these men had had no opportunity to develop them.

Karl-Friedrich was totally undemanding with regard to material things, and was in any case a strong family man and generally at home. He studied physics and chemistry with Nernst and at twenty-four he became assistant to Fritz Haber at the Kaiser-Wilhelm-Institute in Berlin-Dahlem. He took his lecturer's examination in Berlin and as a result of his work there he was offered professorships at Zürich, Harvard, Charkow and Breslau. In the end he accepted a chair at Frankfurt and later was appointed to the Wilhelm Oswald chair at Leipzig and Berlin. When he was thirty he married Grete von Dohnanyi, whose charm and artistic gifts held him captivated throughout his life. In 1938 he was again offered a chair in Chicago, but remained in Germany.

In view of the situation in Berlin and his three sons and small daughter he decided in 1949 to go to Göttingen where he became director of the Max-Planck-Institute of Physical Chemistry. In 1937 he ceased to work in the field of 'heavy water' and from that time onwards applied himself instead to the study of the physical and chemical processes in living organisms. Karl-Friedrich was much beloved by his students and assistants. He hated the régime of National Socialism and gave assistance to those who were persecuted on grounds of race or politics. The exodus of the great Jewish natural scientists such as Born, Courant, Einstein, James Franck, Haber, Landau, Polanyi, Weyl and many others caused him acute pain. He had ties of friendship with many of them and through his work, which achieved world-wide recognition, and his modesty, he also won some very good friends among English and American scientists.

After the murder of our brothers, Klaus and Dietrich, and our brothers-in-law, Hans von Dohnanyi and Rüdiger Schleicher, at the hands of the Gestapo he tried as often as he could manage to be with my parents who had by now grown old. The loss of the four men was very hard for him to bear. Another death which caused him sorrow was that of our uncle, General Paul von Hase, the city commandant of Berlin. On the 20th July, after the attempt on Hitler's life, he had alerted his troops in order to take over the government quarter of the city, and for this he was condemned to death by hanging by Freisler. The pain of this was all the greater since he had also been trying to ease Dietrich's life in prison.

As early as 1946 Karl-Friedrich suffered a heart attack. No brother could have been more concerned about his brothers and sisters than he was. A second heart attack in 1957 brought his life to a premature end at the age of fifty-eight. His colleagues at work wrote: 'In the most difficult times he remained completely objective and upheld truth throughout.'

4

Walter

Walter was born prematurely at seven months on the 10th December 1899. He was fair and blue-eyed like my mother, and slighter in build than Karl-Friedrich. He was no dreamer and very alert. I clearly recall his unceasing preoccupation with his animals. He loved the singing birds and managed to imitate them, and he protected them by making traps to catch cats which he baited with valerian, the horrible smell of which was attractive to the cats.

We little ones were full of admiration for his gymnastic feats on the horizontal and parallel bars. We loved the raft which he made for us to sail on the mountain lakes. We also admired his collection of butterflies, his stones and birds' eggs, the squirrels which he had caught himself, his doves and the animals he kept in aquaria and cages. He loved them all.

I recall how one late afternoon in the room where he kept his animals a kind of non-venomous snake fastened itself so firmly to his thumb with its teeth that he could not shake it off. Although Walter immediately directed a fierce jet of water from the tap onto its head it would not let go and we became frightened. In the end my mother had my father fetched from his consulting-room, a quite unusual occurrence, so that he might teach the snake its manners. I believe that it was given ether.

Walter always knew the hiding places of the small lobsters at the sides of the ponds and he was skilled in catching and cooking them. We were fascinated to see their mud-coloured shells turn bright red when cooked, and we could break open their armour and suck the white and rose-coloured flesh from their claws. I still remember vividly what Walter's hands looked like when he sat at table or played the violin. They were always scrubbed quite clean but were covered all over with the marks of his woodcarving and carpentry at the bench. All three boys had begun their musical training after their sixth birthday and they had a children's trio. But Walter's first love was nature. At Friedrichsbrunn he knew every track through the woods and foresters' path, every trace left by the wild animals, their tracks and hideouts. He would not allow us to walk in the plantations of young fir-trees, but he showed us the special places to look for mushrooms, the slopes where strawberries were to be found, and where the raspberries grew.

At Friedrichsbrunn he was generally out of doors at sunrise. As a devoted hunter he made friends with the foresters everywhere he went. He was an outstanding shot at a very early age, and my father witnessed how he brought down a circling falcon with one shot, but then when the bird fell dead before him he was so shocked that he burst into tears. Hermann Löns' animal books were his passion, and a volume of Brehm's *Animal Life* was generally lying open on his work-table.

When the war broke out in 1914 he was fifteen. He spent a short time in the Boy Scouts but then wanted to subject himself to harder training on his own and on his expeditions he constantly increased the number of sandbags he carried in his rucksack. He wanted to pass his Notabitur* and then enlist straightaway as an officer cadet. In April 1918 Walter joined the fighting forces.

I can still remember that bright May morning in 1918 and the terrible shadow which suddenly blotted it out for us. My father was just in the act of leaving the house to drive to his clinic, and I was on the point of going through the door on my way to school. But when a messenger brought us two telegrams I remained standing in the hall. I saw my father hastily open the envelopes, turn terribly white, go into his study and sink into the chair at his desk where he sat bowed over it with his head resting on both his arms, his face hidden in his hands. I had never seen my father like that. Then I knew what had happened and turned

* A shortened form of the matriculation taken by boys who wanted to join up as quickly as possible.

aside into the dining-room which was empty. A few moments later I saw my father through the half-open door holding onto the banisters as he went up the broad easy stairway which at other times he mounted so lightly to go to the bedroom where my mother was. There he remained for many hours. It was not until the late afternoon that I saw our mother.

At that time my father was fifty years old. About Walter he wrote, 'After a training course at Spandau, Walter was sent back to his field regiment in the spring of 1918 with five other officer cadets. While they were marching to the front on the 22nd April the officer accompanying them made them march in close order on a road that was under fire. A shell fell into the column, killing several and wounding the rest. Walter received several shell splinters in both legs. In the judgement of the doctors this did not at first seem dangerous, but an inflammation developed from which he died eight days later in the field hospital on the 28th April 1918. The warning that his condition was worsening arrived at the same time as the news of his death. From the hospital he had written letters which we only received afterwards, and from these we saw how much he had hoped for a visit. Even today I cannot think of this without reproaching myself for not going to him straightaway in spite of previous reassuring telegrams which explicitly stated that it was unnecessary for me to come.

'Only three hours before his death, after a final operation had been carried out, he dictated a letter to his attendant which I include here: "My dears, today I had the second operation, and I must admit that it went far less pleasantly because the splinters that were removed were deeper. Afterwards I had to have two camphor injections with an interval between them, but I hope that this is the end of the matter. I am using my technique of thinking of other things so as not to think of the pain. There are more interesting things in the world just now than my wounds. The Kemmelberg affair with its possible consequences, and the fact that news has been brought to us that we have taken Ypres, give us much hope. I cannot bring myself to think of my poor regiment at all. The last few days have been so hard for it. How can things be going for the other officer cadets? I am full of longing as I think of you minute by minute throughout the long days and nights. Your loving Walter, still so far away from you."

'The combination of qualities revealed here, the maturity of outlook which prompted him to put himself second, giving first place to his anxieties about his comrades, his regiment and his fatherland, and at the same time a child-like devotion to and longing for his family, were typical of him and probably of many of those destined to be cut off by death in the first years of their young manhood. I am reminded of the student regiments who went to their deaths at Ypres, and whom we miss so much today.'

Forty-five years later in 1963 I myself visited Ypres. At the time the 'last post' was still being sounded every evening on the fortress walls in memory of the Englishmen of the Second Army who had fallen. I also saw the huge memorial which the English had set up in memory of their dead. It is an awe-inspiring sight, completely covered with the names of fifty-five thousand English soldiers. The thirty-five thousand names of those posted missing among the English are engraved on tablets which are placed on the heights of Passchendaele, eastwards from Ypres and not far from the German Langemark memorial. In England I have often heard the same complaint about the flower of youth having fallen there and now being so much missed.

A cousin who was on the general staff made himself responsible for seeing that Walter was brought back to us to Berlin. His burial, which was the first I had ever experienced, is something which I shall never forget: the hearse with the horses decked out in black and all the wreaths, my mother deathly pale and shrouded in a great black mourning veil (all her life she thought that elegance in mourning attire was so ridiculous), my father, my relatives, and all the many silent people dressed in black on the way to the chapel. 'Jerusalem thou city built on high, would to God I were in thee' was the first hymn we sang. Dietrich sat next to me and sang the verses 'loudly and clearly' as Mama always liked us to and as she herself was also able to do. The sermon was preached by our uncle, Hans von Hase. The only words that remain in my memory now are: 'Human nature, what has become of it? In a single hour it returns to the earth, so soon as the winds of death blow into it', from the verses of Paul Gerhardt which I heard for the first time on this occasion, and which sent a cold chill through me as I felt I understood their message. Walter's comrades bore his coffin and the trumpeters played a hymn chosen by my mother. 'What God has done, that is well done. His will is always right. As he initiates all that befalls me, so will I calmly cleave to him.' Although the music of the trumpeters went to my heart I was shocked when I read the passage at home: 'What God has done is well done . . .'. To me it was incomprehensible, and I could not understand why my mother had chosen this hymn.

For almost an entire year I prayed that it might not be Walter whom we had buried but a strange soldier, and that Walter might return. It seemed to me the only way of bringing back any happiness to my parents. For never a day passed without us feeling Walter's loss. After Walter's death it was a long time before my mother recovered her broken strength. Only her faith and the loving care of our father were able to restore her to health.

5

Klaus

The third of us children, Klaus, was born on the 5th January 1901. He was quite different in nature. He had dark eyes and a crop of thick brown hair on his well-shaped head. He found school most distasteful, often arrived late, and became very irritated with his teachers. At an early age he had a marked sense of fairness and could get very hot-tempered if someone gave him less than his due. At sixteen he had to be deprived of his microscope because he sat at it so much that he neglected all his schoolwork and was in danger of being kept down. At seventeen he was appointed orderly to the headquarters at Spaa. There he actually witnessed the flight of Kaiser Wilhelm II to Holland, and described the impression left upon him when, after the last conference with the Kaiser, Hindenburg walked out of the room 'stiff as a statue in his countenance and bearing'.

Klaus was very good hearted and understanding in caring for the sick. He had himself once been so seriously ill after a journey in Africa that we had feared for his life. He always had excellent jokes to tell. His sense of humour lent charm to his mouth and his dark eyes. He played the cello remarkably well but was never satisfied with his efforts. Looking at pictures in museums gave him enormous pleasure and he showed a great love of art in general.

Klaus used to get up late and then liked to eat a hearty break-fast at his ease, loving to indulge in interesting conversation as he did so. At this time of day, however, it was not always as forth-coming as he wished. After lunch he liked to brew some Turkish coffee after grinding the beans himself, to play us records he found interesting or to discuss books he had just read. After the hated days at school were over he studied law. Earlier he had begun to interest himself in economics and social questions, and had done some practical work under Siegmund-Schultze. In contrast to this, the practical side of his training as a young lawyer was abhorrent to him. Here the pedantry or excessive legalism in his seniors vexed him very much.

Klaus was the shortest of the boys, but he was very strong and good at sport. As a child he often used to fight with his brothers. He was also quite fearless. On one occasion when a thief took two fur coats from our hall he chased after him and forced him to give them back.

He loved travelling, and in the course of his life he saw almost all the countries of Europe. He was passionately interested in the ways of life and customs of other nations. During the 1920s he mixed with the Russian émigrés and aroused our enthusiasm for the 'Bluebird', balalaika music and Pavlova's 'Dying Swan'. He used to come to us with Russian recipes and persuaded my mother to give hospitality to an old Russian lady for a considerable period while he was making efforts to learn Russian.

Klaus had a strong critical faculty. In 1930 he published a work which attracted much attention in specialist circles on *Preferential Treatment in Modern International Law*. For a time he was a lawyer with the National Federation of Industry and then became a solicitor and established himself in the Bendlerstrasse in Berlin. And he really did raise heaven and hell when he tried to help someone to obtain his rights. If Klaus wanted to form a judgement on a man whom he was thinking of appointing to some position, the reputation he enjoyed with his colleagues and those who worked under him interested Klaus far more than the recommendations of the man's superiors.

Klaus was very chivalrous and gentle, especially with elderly people. He particularly liked persuading our grandmother to tell him of earlier times, and unlike many young men he felt himself a link in the chain of generations. He was very generous in his presents, loving to give beautiful things that were in some way out of the ordinary. He was well groomed and wore a hat, scarf and gloves, often carrying an umbrella as well, though we brothers and sisters used to tease him about this.

At the age of twenty-nine he married Emmi Delbrück, the

youngest daughter of Professor Hans Delbrück, the historian. He had known her from childhood days and was a very close friend of her brother, Justus Delbrück. They had a daughter and two sons.

He was extremely interested in politics and right from the outset he was a resolute opponent of National Socialism on the grounds that it was evil and 'sub-standard' in every way. His fine sense of justice, which he had developed at an early stage, was outraged by it beyond all bounds. With shame and fury he described how a 'non-Aryan' advocate who had been dismissed came into the court, unbuckled his wooden leg and threw it on the table with the words, 'That is the thanks of the fatherland!' When Eberhard Bethge writes, 'From shame and love Christians and non-Christians alike rose in revolt', this also applied to Klaus. Everything that he held dear was at stake, and at that time he held the view that the evil should be nipped in the bud. He had a good nose for what was sham or corrupt and could react passionately against meanness. In the resistance he collaborated with the von Harnack and Leuschner group and with his friends, Nikolaus von Halem and Otto John.

Klaus had premonitions of death. He often feared that in their resistance to the Hitler régime our family would come to an unhappy end. In 1937 when my husband and I wanted to arrive at an arrangement with him he remarked, 'Yes, in the Spring ... if we are not already pushing up the daisies by then!', and on another occasion he said to me, 'You will see, we shall all come to the scaffold yet!'

Klaus did not flee when his arrest was imminent although he could have had time to do so and an aeroplane was available— at that time he was legal adviser to Lufthansa—because he was anxious lest after his flight reprisals would be taken against other members of his family and friends.

Klaus contemplated taking his own life. My sister, Ursula Schleicher, was able to dissuade him from this course. Later, when Klaus was tortured by the Gestapo, she often asked herself whether she had done right in this. On the 2nd February 1945 Klaus was condemned to death by the so-called 'People's Court' together with our brother-in-law, Rüdiger Schleicher, who was a high civil servant in the Air Ministry and had been held prisoner with Klaus in the Moabit Prison since October 1944.

His fellow prisoner, Eberhard Bethge, said of Klaus, 'On the evening of his sentence as he stood upright at the cell door greeting us, he managed to convey the message that we should hold firm and maintain our dignity'. To his parents he wrote: 'In any case it is a much simpler task to die than to live on in times of such confusion. This is why those to whom death has been allotted as their task have always been considered blessed. ... On this ride* between death and the devil, death is a noble companion. However it may turn out I have been spared an unworthy fate.' Before his sentence of death was published Klaus wrote down on a scrap of paper: 'I am not afraid of being hanged, but I do not want to see these faces again ... so much depravity—I would much rather die than see these faces again. I have seen the devil. That is something of which I cannot rid my mind.'

When my brother Karl-Friedrich visited him in the prison after the sentence had been promulgated Klaus told him that he had the Matthew Passion on his folding table. Karl-Friedrich was impressed that he could hear music just by reading the score. Klaus said, 'But the words too, the words!' His wife was still able to speak with him a few more times. He left behind some beautiful letters to her and his three children, and these have been included in several collections of letters of the twentieth century.

On the 24th April 1945 their house was burnt down. But the children were safely evacuated and, thank God, Emmi Bonhoeffer was able to free herself from the blocked cellar. On the 23rd April 1945, shortly before the conquest of Berlin, Klaus was taken away at night by the S.S. and shot from behind.

His wife was enabled to bear this terrible fate of his because of the great welfare work for refugees which she built up in Schleswig-Holstein. She put her innate practical energy and imagination at the service of her fellow men and thus lived on in the spirit in which her husband had died.

* Klaus here refers to Albrecht Dürer's picture, 'Knight, Death and Devil'.

6

Ursula

Ursula was born in May 1902. Even as a little girl she was beautiful with her clear-cut features, her very large, dark eyes and her long, brown plaits. She did not play our rough games with us, but preferred to look after her dolls or do something quiet and useful, and at fourteen she was already very skilled in household matters. Ursel was extremely conscientious at school, too, and in general she was always a little too serious for her age. She found it horrible that Walter shot sparrows, and wept when some blood from the sparrows fell on her dress. But she loved her 'little gatherings' with friends and needlework. Later she developed a good alto voice.

After she had finished school she went to the Pestalozzi-Fröbel-House and then to Fräulein von Gierkes' Youth Centre. She wanted to become a social worker and began her training, but became engaged before she had completed it. At the age of twenty-one she married Rüdiger Schleicher, who was a high civil servant in the Air Ministry at the time. In the First World War he had been seriously wounded, and still often suffered greatly with the wound in his leg.

A great harmony emanated from Ursel. She and Rüdiger had four children and everyone enjoyed their charming family life. Rüdiger was a very good violinist and music was infinitely important to him. The sound of music was almost always to be heard issuing from that hospitable house. This was until the great disaster fell upon it: the failure of the attempt on Hitler's life on the 20th July 1944, led to Rüdiger's being imprisoned in the

Moabit Prison and being brought before Hitler's 'People's Court' where Freisler condemned him to death together with my brother Klaus on the 2nd February 1945.

With such a womanly heart as she had, Ursula had always worried a great deal about her husband and children. She had never viewed life through rose-tinted spectacles. She always proved herself in emergencies and actually gave shelter to Jews during the period of persecution, even though she placed herself in danger by doing so. She was able to visit Rüdiger a number of times during his time of imprisonment and brought him what she could in his isolation cell, even his violin which lightened the cruelties of his captivity to some extent. When he wanted to play, the warder, who liked to listen, would undo his chains.

On the night of 22nd-23rd April 1945, when Berlin was already under fire from the Russians, Rüdiger Schleicher, my brother Klaus, and a few other prisoners were informed that they would be moved and perhaps even set free. Instead of this they were brought out with certain other prisoners, each of them being followed by an S.S. man with an automatic pistol. In the open district around Ulap they were suddenly pressed against a wall and all were murdered with a shot through the back of the neck. A survivor, who had not been mortally wounded but who pretended to be dead, was able a little later to save himself and describe how the murder was committed. The victims were buried in a bomb crater along with other war dead.

It was the last death sentence issued by Freisler. At this time an event took place which may seem incredible to all who read about it, but which is, nevertheless, true. The day after the death sentence a brother of Rüdiger Schleicher's had come from Stuttgart to Berlin with a petition for mercy on Rüdiger's behalf and was on the way to Thierack, the Minister of Justice, in order to lay it before him. Just then, in broad daylight, a devastating bombing raid fell upon Berlin, and Freisler, the president of the 'People's Court', was struck down. A doctor was called for and fate decreed that it should be precisely Rüdiger Schleicher's brother who, as senior staff doctor, was brought to Freisler. He could only confirm the fact of death but he refused to issue the certificate of death until he had been allowed to see Thierack. Thierack is said to have been taken aback at this unprecedented coincidence. He promised Rolf Schleicher that the execution would be postponed and that when a petition for clemency had been submitted the sentence would be reviewed.

In the meantime Ursel had been able to have a brief interview with her husband. Rolf Schleicher came to her with the words, 'The scoundrel is dead'.

Ursel had long been a prey to the most dreadful anxieties, the more so since Rüdiger had never been able to tell even a necessary lie. Now the murder of her husband had a terrible effect on her. It was a long time before she recovered from a heart attack. Yet surely we can apply to Ursula those famous words which run, 'What lies in the future and is still distant fills her fearful heart with anxiety. But what is a present and unalterable fact she bears with resignation'.

The problem then was how to provide the children with an education. Her eldest daughter had married Dietrich's friend, Pastor Eberhard Bethge. Her son returned from the war and read physical chemistry while her other daughters began to read languages and medicine. After Ursula's children had all married she exchanged her house in Berlin, the roof of which had been burnt out in 1945, for a small pretty modern house which she had built at Hamburg, next door to Professor Ritschl and his wife, in whom she had found a most loyal friend. Today she has twelve grandchildren who often visit her and learn from her practical wisdom and experience. Through them she remains in contact with the new world, and for their welfare she once more plans and works.

7

Christel

Christel was born in 1903 and was next in age to Ursula. Thus the family of children as a whole fell into three groups: 'the three big boys', 'the two girls', 'the twins'. 'The twins' were subsequently numbered with Susi, the youngest, to constitute 'the three little ones' so as not to isolate her—though we twins were offended by this.

Dolls meant nothing to Christel, and with her interest in animals she was particularly close to Walter. She busied herself with him in looking after his squirrels and turtle doves, his collection of butterflies and the cages and aquaria which she made her hobby together with him. Like him she was captivated by all aspects of forest life at Friedrichsbrunn. She loved to sit on the shooting stand with Walter and the forester. She knew the haunts of the roe deer and wild boar, and was also at an early age a very ambitious shot, first, it must be admitted, with a peashooter and later with an airgun.

When Walter died Christel lost her childhood world. At his death she was fifteen. Since she was anxious to study zoology later on she went to the Grunewald school when she was sixteen. Here her objectivity and active interests were respected by teachers and fellow pupils alike. She hated unnecessary verbiage and was already precise in her use of words. She loved controversies and was as good at these as the boys. She was extremely reserved, but could be very witty. Her quick-wittedness, combined with her humour, were great fun. While she was still in the upper fifth, Christel came to know the boy to whom she was later to become engaged, Hans von Dohnanyi. He was two years older than she was and at that time about to take his matriculation. Probably they already then made up their minds to marry one day.

I particularly liked to hear Christel sing. The songs she sang especially well were the Mignon *Lieder* and also the other Goethe-Beethoven *Lieder*. Christel had not much voice but she sang very sensitively. She spent only a few semesters reading zoology and did not complete her course as she married Hans von Dohnanyi in 1925 and accompanied him to Hamburg. Hans von Dohnanyi was extraordinarily gifted as a lawyer and also in the arts. His energy and capacity for work were astounding, and he was never ill. With all this he had great personal charm. After he had passed his final law examinations he took up an academic post as assistant at the Institute for Foreign Affairs under Professor Mendelssohn-Bartholdy. Subsequently, in 1929, he became personal assistant to the Ministers of State for Justice, Koch-Weser, Bredt and Joel. He stayed on when Gürtner was appointed to this post, and it was with his agreement that as early as 1933 he began to work in the resistance to Hitler. After the removal of General von Fritsch had been brought about by the use of base and defamatory methods, Dohnanyi's relations with General von Beck, at that time Chief of the General Staff, grew closer.

In 1937 Hitler held a secret conference in which he gave the General Staff clearly to understand that he would impose his 'territorial claims' by force. From this time onwards General von Beck strove with all his energies to rouse the generals to revolt and to resist Hitler's invasion plans, but in vain. In May 1938 Hitler informed the government and the General Staff that he was about to occupy Czechoslovakia. Again it was von Beck who refused to subject his conscience to the will of Hitler and who, in the strongest possible terms, reminded General Brauchitsch, the Commander-in-Chief of the armed forces, of his duty to resist this command. But all von Beck's efforts and those of his friends, General Oster and the Chiefs of Defence, Canaris and Dohnanyi, were in vain. The invasion of Czechoslovakia took place. In August von Beck resigned from his post but thenceforward he worked all the more energetically with Canaris, Oster, Dohnanyi and certain other like-minded officers and civilians in the resistance to Hitler's régime. When Dohnanyi did not enter the party, Freisler and Bormann, who were jealous, denounced him. As a result he left this service and came to Leipzig as a judge at the Supreme Court for civil and penal cases, but he maintained contact with Admiral Canaris who became Head of German Military Counter-Intelligence service in the O.K.W.* in 1938, and also with General Oster and von Hassel.

Christel first developed her political interests in connection with the political work of her husband. It was her sense of justice and decency, her abhorrence of so much crime and meanness, which drew her so strongly into the resistance to Hitler. She knew how to keep silence and thus at a later stage was kept informed about the steps undertaken in the political sphere by Canaris, Oster and Dohnanyi.

She was arrested in 1943, together with my brother Dietrich and her husband, and sent to a women's prison where women guilty of serious offences were placed. Thank God my father succeeded in obtaining Christel's release through the assistance of an old friend of his student days. Her husband was first sent to the Officers' Prison and later to the concentration camp at Sachsenhausen, where he was subjected to unspeakable tortures. Ever since 1933 Hans von Dohnanyi had been assembling a 'chronicle' of all the criminal actions of the leading figures in the party. Concerning this, my sister Christel von Dohnanyi writes as follows: 'There is hardly a crime that has not been recorded in this "chronicle", from the murders and attempted murders in the concentration camps, the atrocities in these camps which have in the meantime become generally known, to the widespread currency smuggling of the gauleiters and the disgusting obscenities within the Hitler Youth and S.A. leadership. My husband added to and completed this material over a number of years. It included speeches by Hitler, accounts of the treatment of prisoners of war, films of the atrocities in Poland, the initial causes of the "bloody Sunday" of Bromberg, instructions by Goebbels for the pogroms of the Jews and further material of a similar kind. My husband was convinced that these accounts could be supplemented at will, given the opportunity, by those who had knowledge of similar crimes in other departments. In view of this he told me these records should suffice to open the

* Oberkommando der Wehrmacht, the Army High Command.

eyes of anyone willing to discern the truth about Hitler and his régime'. Right from the outset General von Beck took a great interest in these records in order to be able to demonstrate later on that the conspiracy against Hitler did not begin merely when the war was accounted as lost.

No words of mine can describe how terrible and harrowing this time was for Christel. Her husband had been so tenderly devoted to her and the unison between them and their harmony of thought and action made it a marriage quite out of the ordinary. The Gestapo described Hans von Dohnanyi as 'the intellectual head of the movement to overthrow the Fuehrer'. Pastor Pölchau, who visited him in prison, recorded: 'I found a man who was suffering in body but composed and extraordinarily impressive. Such services as I could do him were only slight.'

The tasks that were laid upon Christel were terrible. Her husband asked her to smuggle in some diphtheria bacilli to him which he wanted to take in order to delay his trial. Christel sent them to him. As a result he became severely crippled and at first lost the ability to walk. In April 1945 Hans von Dohnanyi was executed at Sachsenhausen. Before he came to Sachsenhausen, Christel had been able to visit him occasionally with the children —Professor Sauerbruch had taken Hans von Dohnanyi into his clinic and for a long time guarded him like a lion against the Gestapo—and had been able to discuss the most important matters with him.

At that time their children were eighteen, sixteen, and fifteen years old. Thenceforward, Christel lived only for them and the relationship between her and the children was particularly close. But she never got over her terrible suffering and no one could help her. She did not show her feelings. Her great self-discipline was always her strongest characteristic. But she did not make life any easier for herself thereby.

Christel still took pleasure in the gifts with which her children were endowed and in the interest which her sons brought to the professions which they later entered, as also in the recognition which they won in them. She had a further loss in a beloved daughter-in-law, and although she had lived for a long period in the family of her daughter, Bärbel, she then went to her son in order to act as mother to her grandson.

Christel prized beautiful things and probably, too, enjoyed

elegance, but her real respect was reserved for frugality and simplicity of life. At fifty-three she suffered a heart attack, and although she recovered she still continued to suffer from its effects.

It was characteristic of her that right up to her death she enjoyed going for walks in the forest every day for hours on end, for, without her husband, household matters no longer meant anything to her. In the final years of her illness she came to know a Dr Külper in a sanatorium in Kassel. He had come to know of what she had endured through the writings of Dietrich. He was able to perceive her suffering and her interior loneliness. He devoted almost his entire day to her and accompanied her daily for many hours on her walks, read her all the books which interested her and talked with her about all those matters which for so long she had been unable to discuss for want of anyone to talk to. She took great pleasure in all this. Six months before her death she wrote to me: 'The children are touching, but after all they have their professions and their households, I think that is more than enough. I cannot decide whether the cure has been of any help. If the kind doctor, who is himself recovering from an illness, were not here I would be in a bad way.'

Under the influence of Dr Külper her feelings about what she had endured underwent a change. Dr Külper had himself been seriously ill. His wide reading, his understanding and his readiness to help did her good. She often spoke quite openly with him, although to others she hardly ever mentioned the human and political problems of those terrible times, which still occupied her innermost thoughts. These conversations relieved her spirit. It was Dr Külper who stood at her side when, at sixty-one, Christel died unexpectedly from another heart attack. This man, who so well put into practice the Christian principle of love of neighbour, had understood how to induce her to call her own scepticism into question.

8

Dietrich

I find it most difficult to give a picture of Dietrich. 'How shall I praise and yet remain moderate, sparing no detail lest my picture of you falls short of the truth?' Whether the fact that I was his twin has anything to do with the matter I am unable to say. At all events the unity which existed between myself and my elder brothers and my sisters was different in kind from the unity of my relationship with my twin brother, Dietrich.

Dietrich entered the world on the 4th February 1906, ten minutes before me, and during our childhood he liked proudly to emphasize the fact that he had arrived before me. He was blue-eyed, sturdy, and equipped with a great crop of flaxen hair. At four years old he asked my mother, 'Does the good God love the chimney sweep too?' and 'Does God, too, sit down to lunch?'

Inevitably we were a team. It was taken for granted that either of us would say to the other, 'Come on', when some new adventure or activity presented itself. When we took part in ball games or games of soldiers with other children we were never on opposite sides, always united, though to a slight extent I allowed him to take the lead. Whenever Dietrich was 'dreadfully thirsty' or found it 'dreadfully hot', or during the war in 1917, felt 'dreadfully hungry' or had a 'dreadful tummy-ache', I always came to know of it.

For all his exuberance and strength, Dietrich was a sensitive child and, moreover, did not easily make friends at school. Admittedly he had his own brothers and sisters as his playmates.

From eight to ten years old Dietrich and I slept in the same room, and when we were in bed at night we used to have earnest discussions about death and eternal life. The war of 1914 had broken out and we heard of the deaths of our big cousins and some of the fathers of our classmates. And so in the evenings after prayers and hymn singing, in which our mother always took part when she was in the house, we used to lie awake for a long time and try to imagine to ourselves what it must be like to be dead and to have entered upon eternal life. We used to make special efforts to draw a little nearer every evening to eternity by resolving to think only of the word 'eternity' and not to admit any other thought to our minds. This eternity seemed to us very long and uncanny. After concentrating intently for a long time our heads often used to swim. We staunchly kept up this self-imposed exercise for a long time. We were very dependent upon one another and each wanted to be the last to call out a final 'goodnight' to the other. I remember how these 'goodnights' used to be endlessly tossed to and fro and how difficult we often found it to tear ourselves from sleep in order to reply to them. All this was an absolute secret between us twins.

Dietrich was a chivalrous boy. He used to carry anything that was too heavy for his sisters, and when we had to read from the same book he used to push it closer to me. In general he was always kind and helpful when he was asked to do anything.

As a child Dietrich did find some things frightening, and to that extent his first days at the Friedrich-Werder school in 1913 turned out to be rather difficult ones. On the way to school he had to cross a large bridge and because of this he was reluctant to make the journey alone. The first few times, therefore, he had to be accompanied. The grown-up accompanying him walked on the opposite side of the road in order not to shame him before his companions. Finally he overcame this fear.

At Friedrichsbrunn in our second home we enjoyed all the delights of the mountains and woods together. We could invite friends and cousins to Friedrichsbrunn. But Dietrich did not want to bring any of his classmates home. He still did not have any special friends, but he used to be glad when our cousin Hans Christoph von Hase, who was the same age as ourselves, was able to come with us. In the large garden at Friedrichsbrunn we were free to do as we liked. We used to creep about in the glades of the pinewoods and eagerly search for mushrooms, which we learned to recognize with great accuracy. It could send Dietrich into transports of joy when he found a particularly fine one. Another memory which I find unforgettable is how sweet Dietrich used to be when we gathered berries on the hot summer slopes. He used to fill my basket with the raspberries he had picked with such toil himself so that I might not have less than he, and in steep places he used to reach out his hand to help me.

In the evenings the village children, too, would take part in general ball games in our big meadow. This was something that Dietrich loved especially. At games he was not without ambition but absolutely fair, whereas the others sometimes liked to cheat. One day he returned home from a game wearing a victor's crown, but was laughed at for this ostentation by our big brothers so that he took off the garland with the utmost embarrassment. On expeditions through the Harz Mountains Dietrich always liked us to make a halt as soon as we reached Halberstadt or Quedlinburg so that he could take another look at the large churches. He used to stand there full of reverence, wondering and speculating as to who lay buried here. He already knew all sorts of details about the history of these towns.

At eight years old Dietrich discovered the joys of music, and every Saturday evening our parents used to encourage him to give a piano recital. He became extremely skilled at playing from sight, and was soon asked to accompany the cello and violin and his sisters when they sang. He particularly liked to accompany our mother when she sang the Gellert-Beethoven psalms or the Cornelius *Lieder* on Christmas eve. Dietrich was a most sensitive accompanist and here, too, his good character showed—he was always anxious to cover over the mistakes of the other players and to spare them any embarrassment. He was most patient and often kept up his accompaniment for hours so that sometimes he did not have time for his own piano practice, although for a while he actually thought of becoming a pianist. In the end he had the good judgement to realize that he would not be good enough at the piano to make music his profession.

When he was about fourteen he composed a setting for the psalm 'Why art thou cast down, O my soul? And why art thou disquieted in me? Hope thou in God for I shall yet praise him for the help of his countenance'. At that time, too, he attempted to compose a trio-setting for Schubert's song *Gute Ruh*. Unfortunately neither of these has survived. On his seventeenth birthday I made an inscription for him, decorating it with my paintbrush in three colours, of Tersteegen's verses,

> *Each day tells the other*
> *My life is but a journey*
> *to great and endless life.*
> *O sweetness of eternity,*
> *May my heart grow to love thee;*
> *My home is not here in time's strife.*

Dietrich had asked me for this and he was very pleased with it and hung it up in his room.

He was happy at the Grunewald School and had a good relationship with his teachers and fellow pupils even though here, too, he did not make any particular friend. At fifteen we received confirmation together, and at that time Dietrich had already decided to study theology.

Dietrich loved festive occasions. These festivals and balls which we held had acquired a certain reputation. Evidently they were never boring. Perhaps it was the blend of artistic and academic traditions which imparted such charm to the atmosphere of our family home and attracted so many individuals thither by the most varied paths. Professors Delbrück, Harnack, Hertwig, Planck, His, Hildebrand and their families lived in the neighbourhood, and the young people, together with the young doctors from the hospital, musicians, theologians and jurists held balls and celebrated birthdays and examination results with us at our house. Dietrich had inherited from our mother that blessed talent of finding happiness in giving hospitality and making others feel at home.

The closeness between Dietrich and myself still survived even when externally speaking our paths led in different directions. For the time came for Dietrich to commence his theological studies, while in my case my engagement and then marriage meant that my life was mainly taken up with my husband and children.

After a few preliminary semesters of theological study at

Tübingen, Dietrich continued his studies at Berlin. It was here that his first really close friendship began. It was with a fellow student of theology, Franz Hildebrandt, who later became professor of theology at Drew University in the United States. As early as 1927 Dietrich graduated with a thesis on *Sanctorium Communio* under R. Seeberg. I remember how he worked at his standing desk yet always allowed himself to be interrupted when I came into my parents' garden in the mornings with the perambulator in which his godchild Marianne lay. In 1928 Dietrich passed his first theological examination and one month later he went as chaplain to the German congregation in Barcelona. He wrote many letters to us from Spain, and tried to induce us to make a visit there in order to show us all its beauties. Even the bullfights fascinated him. It was from Barcelona that he wrote us the following two letters:

Barcelona   17.3.1928

Dear Sabine,

Many thanks for your card. You are complaining a bit that you hear so little from me. Didn't you get my last letter? If not, I'm sorry, I must admit that at the moment I am very busy with social engagements. Last week every afternoon and all my evenings were taken up with visiting or invitations, and from different people every time. In the afternoons I am at the minister's house and work for the welfare organizations, the consulting hours for these being in the morning. I find the work very interesting because in it one comes across every variety of people, united only in one point: that all of them are without money. You can see for yourself, therefore, that I do not have all that much time to write.

In your last letter you say that you are surprised that I am in a 'choral society' and you probably believe that I spend my evenings singing '*Gott grüsse dich*'. Now, this isn't altogether true (in any case my part in the affair is to play the piano). At the same time I meet all kinds of people in this choral society. The majority are business people who have worked their way up over the years until they have acquired a certain degree of prosperity. This is, so to say, a prerequisite for being admitted to this group, since it is a general

41

rule here that the people only mix with those who are their financial equals, regardless of what class they belong to in terms of education. Individuals like us have the advantage in that people accept us everywhere and actually like to see us because of our connection with the Church. It strikes me again and again that those who come out of Germany prompted by the so-called lust for adventure and bold enterprises are infernally materialistic in outlook and have not acquired any other interests through their stay abroad. This also applies to the teachers. In time I shall become well acquainted with the congregation, especially with the children and also to some extent with the families.

At the moment I have very little time for work on my own account. When you get this letter it will be six weeks since I have left home. Time flies! When are you coming to Italy? Do make a journey through Corsica to Mallorca so that I can come and visit you there. This would be quite splendid! Enough! I must go out again now, and then do some work for tomorrow (Sunday).

May all go well with you. I think of you all so often.

Yours, Dietrich

Barcelona   22.4.1928

Dear Sabine,

Many thanks for your last letter. While you were spending your time so peaceably looking for Easter eggs I have been to a bullfight with Klaus and another of my acquaintances. Probably Klaus has in fact already given you a detailed account of it. I was quite astonished how much more cold-bloodedly I reacted to the affair the second time than the first, and I must say that after all I can have some remote inkling of the fact that there is a certain fascination in the whole thing which makes some acquire a passion for it. With every bull one becomes quicker at seeing beyond the element of sensationalism and cruelty. This may in fact be due to a progressive 'brutalization', but it does allow one to achieve a closer insight into the nature of the business, and to bring more understanding to bear upon it. Apart from this, the swing from 'Hosanna' to 'Crucify him!' has never been brought home to me so vividly as in the positively senseless roaring of the crowd when the torero makes a good pass and the equally senseless screaming and whistling which follow immediately upon this when some kind of bad luck befalls the same torero. The fickleness which is characteristic of the voice of the masses is so extreme that they applaud the bull instead of the torero if, for instance, the latter is considered to be faint-hearted or if (something which is in fact wholly understandable) his courage fails him even for a moment.

You will also already have heard about Montserrat so I will briefly tell you a little more, since that is what you want, about everyday matters. During the absence of the pastor I have had to hold the interviews for the welfare organization alone every morning from nine to eleven. For the most part this is not a very enjoyable beginning to the day, even though it is quite instructive and enlightening. Actually one is constantly being lied to—something which one only finds out afterwards—and there is seldom a case in which one gives help really willingly or with a good conscience, and that is a great pity.

After these interviews I am in theory free for the day. But this is only 'in theory', for in practice the way things turn out for the most part is that I only arrive home at one o'clock in the morning from some function or meeting I have been invited to and find that once more I have not managed to do any writing or reading or learning Spanish or done any other kind of work. Most of the time is spent in visiting members of the congregation, both the healthy and the sick, and here, especially in the latter cases, one does have very rewarding experiences. If there is a free afternoon or evening one likes to go into the city or to a café to have a little change of scene. Even there one generally meets some acquaintance or other with whom one then spends two or three hours in chatting, so that by the time this is over it is either time for dinner, i.e. 8.30 p.m. or time to go to bed, i.e. here 1-1.30 a.m.

In order to take part in some music I go to the choral society on Mondays where I am the piano player. I don't play much at home, and at other times only play in recitals. I don't practise seriously with others. This, too, is something for which the people here are too dull-witted, for the people here really are dull-witted utterly and beyond all measure, old and young alike. Dull-witted, that is to say, in all matters apart from their businesses. At the same time they are pleasant enough and one gets on very well with them. In this society one very soon blunts one's academic horns. The situation is such that it is exceptional for a boy of fourteen or upwards to have any kind of real interest to pursue. Once they have got beyond the stage of boys' adventure stories they read magazines and do gym. Apart from that the Basque ball game and tennis take up the rest of the time in which a boy might be forming ideas. A typical instance occurred recently when a boy who has just been confirmed looked at me in utter amazement and quite at a loss when I asked him whether he had had any difficulties with the apostles' creed during his confirmation instruction. What did I mean? he asked, Was there any kind of doubt about it? Anything which does not absolutely have to be thought out is thrust aside. The worst of fates would be to have one idea too many.

This is a picture of my present life. I like being here and find it interesting. Whether I can stand it for longer than one year admittedly is something which I don't know yet. Now I must conclude. Tomorrow we start off on the journey. Give Grandmama my love and tell her to be sure to write too, very soon.

Today it is doing its utmost to pour with rain. Is there snow where you are? I hope it is better towards the south. Rüdiger's letter gave me special pleasure. Please thank him with all my heart.

All best wishes to you three,

Your loving Dietrich

My parents and Klaus visited Dietrich in Barcelona. He remained there for one year. In 1930 he passed the further examination which he had to take. His intense concentration upon his work soon bore fruit. In that same year he wrote the thesis for his lecturer's examination. The subject was 'Act and Being'. Still in the same month he gave his inaugural lecture on 'The Question of Man in Current Philosophy and Theology'.

In 1930 he then went as an exchange student for nine months to the Union Theological Seminary at New York. When he returned from the States he also attended Karl Barth's lectures on theology at Bonn for some weeks. In 1931 he was very busy indeed. He was now a lecturer in the faculty of theology at the University of Berlin and simultaneously chaplain to the students at the Technical University. In the same year he was instructing his confirmation class in the Zionskirche. I accompanied my mother to the confirmation of those whom Dietrich had pre-pared. We were very moved by the service and by Dietrich's sermon. Here for the first time I saw Dietrich in his gown.

Immediately after Hitler had seized power, Dietrich gave some talks on the radio in which he showed himself quite decisively opposed to National Socialism. He remarked to me that if the Aryan Clauses* were put into force in the Church then 'some-thing exceedingly strong' would have to be done. Accordingly as early as the 1st February 1933 Dietrich gave a broadcast address on the subject of 'The Fuehrer and the Individual in the Younger Generation'. We were listening to his address on the radio and witnessed how his message was suddenly interrupted. Diet-rich had said, 'The individual man, and in particular the young man, will feel the need to submit himself to the authority of a leader (Fuehrer) to the extent that he feels that he himself is not mature enough, strong enough or responsible enough to realize for himself the claims imposed by this authority. The leader (Fuehrer) will have to be responsible enough to be aware of these clear limitations to his authority. He must view his function from its true basis in reality. If he interprets it in any other sense, if he fails to give clear guidance constantly and repeatedly to his follower with regard to the limitations of his own function and with regard to the deepest personal responsibility which that follower has, then the image of the leader (Fuehrer) will degenerate into that of the seducer (*Verfuehrer*) . . .'

Dietrich was indignant at the sudden breaking off of his ad-dress. But the *Kreuz* newspaper printed it as an article almost without alteration and later he found it possible to give the same address once more in an expanded form to the Berlin Political University. When the Aryan Clauses were introduced Dietrich wrote to Karl Barth as follows:

* These clauses would debar 'non-Aryan' Christians from the Ministry, even the already-ordained pastors.

'You have stated that any Church which introduced the Aryan Clauses ceases thereby to be a Christian Church. A large section of these ministers is certainly at one with you in this opinion. Now what we have expected has come to pass, and I ask you in the name of many friends, ministers and students to let us know whether you consider it possible to remain in a Church which has ceased to be a Christian Church . . .'

Still in the same month Dietrich wrote an article entitled 'The Church in Face of the Jewish Question'. Here he stated that it is the task of Christian preaching to give clear expression to the truth that 'here, where Jew and German stand together under the word of God, is the Church. Here the question is put to the proof whether the Church still is the Church or not'. To the neutrals who took refuge in the liturgy Dietrich exclaimed: 'Only he who cries out on behalf of the Jews can legitimately sing Gregorian.' To the brethren who were willing to submit in order to obtain a post as pastor he said: 'A single act of obedience carries more credibility than a hundred sermons delivered by a disobedient pastor.'

As early as 1933 Dietrich foresaw that a situation was destined to arise which would impose upon the Church the inescapable duty 'not merely of binding up the wounds of the victim beneath the wheel but of herself putting a spoke in that same wheel'. Later in 1933 Dietrich decided to take over as pastor to the German Communities of St Paul and Sydenham. His purpose was to turn his back on the National Socialist leadership of the Church as a protest.

In St Paul's Whitechapel and Sydenham Dietrich preached two sermons on Sundays. Hitherto he had never exercised the full functions customary for a minister officially appointed to a congregation and for this reason Rieger, the pastor of St George's Church in London, supposed that it would give Dietrich a great deal to do. 'He believed that he had recognized that a community held together by the word of God must be nothing else than "Christ existing in community form" and that the sermon has to be "Christ as preached". And now, believing this, he felt the burden of the Sunday preaching doubly severe and a heavy responsibility.'

1. Paula Bonhoeffer with her eight children in 1909. Left to right (standing): Christine, Klaus, Ursula, Karl-Friedrich, Walter; left to right (sitting): Sabine, Paula Bonhoeffer with baby Susanne, Dietrich

2. Karl Bonhoeffer

3. Birkenwäldchen 7, the house at Breslau where the twins were born in 1906

4. The seven oldest Bonhoeffer children in the garden at Breslau in 1909

Community visiting was of prime importance for Dietrich. On one occasion he had gone to a film with Pastor Rieger. The two had planned to stay together and have dinner with one an- other afterwards. But in the middle of an extremely exciting episode he whispered to Rieger that he had just remembered that he had to visit a member of the community, and hastily disappeared. He took the duties of the ministry to the refugees from the Third Reich very seriously. Rieger wrote, 'Bonhoeffer seldom said anything about himself. When he was asked about the thesis he had written for his degree he evaded the question remarking, in a way that almost seemed to parry it, "that it is a very theoretical book." I never heard him play the piano. He never used his abilities as a pianist to give recitals to others. . . . Only very seldom did he "come out of himself" as when, quite incidentally, he told us that occasionally anthroposophist publi- cations had given him much thought or that a stay in a church at Rome had been a strong temptation to him to become a Catholic or when . . . he expressed the opinion that it must be terrible to be forty years old—that was something he would never experience. . . . On one occasion mention was made of the fact that in some Catholic communities prayers were offered for those of the Confessing Church who were imprisoned or perse- cuted. And when some people said that they saw "nothing special" in this Bonhoeffer reacted sharply with the remark, "to me it is no matter of indifference that someone is praying for me!" '

In April 1939, when Rieger and Dietrich were travelling to Germany, Rieger could not repress his joy as a German returning from abroad, but Dietrich remarked to him, 'We are just coming into a fine prison'. Dietrich maintained a frequent and very warm contact with the Bishop of Chichester, both in person and by letter. At that time they were both greatly concerned about the evil activities in the Church of the so-called 'German Christians'.

During the London period, my parents often spoke with Dietrich on the telephone. Mama had sent him a housekeeper and contributed furniture, a grand piano and all sorts of house- hold goods which he needed for his pastor's house at Forest Hill. He soon bought a young St Bernard dog as well. He only liked dogs which were perfectly trained and obeyed him, and he had a special liking for St Bernards. But unfortunately his St

c

The Bonhoeffers

Bernard was run over in London and Dietrich was very sad about it.

Barth was very annoyed with him for going to London, and impressed upon him very deeply that he must return home to Germany again in order to support the Confessing Church. In 1935 Dietrich left London once more and took over the Preachers' Seminary of the Confessing Church at Finkenwalde. Moreover, he continued this work even when it was declared illegal by the National Socialist government. At this time Eberhard Bethge first met him, and he has left the following impression of him:

'It was in 1935 on the yellow sandy shore of the Baltic that I first met Dietrich Bonhoeffer: a tall, powerfully built man of hardly thirty years, with lively blue eyes, a sensitive but controlled mouth and rather relaxed movements. He revealed himself to be an extremely unconventional guide to this collection of aspiring ministers. When the sun shone to any extent upon the bright shore its message could not go unheeded. Only very reluctantly and very rarely did he allow himself to lose in the games we played on the shore.... Gradually, but more and more willingly, we let ourselves be introduced to the subject of human freedom. Properly speaking this was the last thing we had envisaged as part of our training in an illegal seminary for pastors at this time of furious conflict. Certainly we argued energetically against the teachings of the German Christians. But in this we evinced the same furious zeal and dogged earnestness as our opponents. Bonhoeffer, on the other hand, though probably more uncompromising than anyone, had from the outset this quite different and higher dimension of personal freedom, and he could impart it in a way that was irresistible.'

Dietrich unreservedly made a place for my husband in the union which existed between us as brother and sister, and that, too, in very high degree, especially as the Hitler régime had brought personal and professional difficulties to Gert. Dietrich gave him his immediate and decisive support just as, as a matter of principle, Dietrich believed that the Church had a duty to stand up for those who had been deprived of their rights and forced to keep silence. It was not enough for him that the

Church should preach peace and strive to maintain her own position.

During those unedifying years which followed upon Hitler's seizure of power we were still living at Göttingen. Dietrich often visited us there with his friend, Franz Hildebrandt, the assistant preacher to Niemöller, and later with Eberhard Bethge. Our relationship with Dietrich's friends was extremely cordial. There were always fine weeks with long walks in the woods and also games of tennis. Dietrich liked to work on our sunny veranda and in the evenings we had many discussions about politics, the Church's struggle, and the future which was so impenetrable to us. Sometimes, too, we listened to music, and sometimes Dietrich or Franz Hildebrandt played something on our grand piano. In the evening he often spoke to our parents in Berlin on the telephone, but even at that time code words were often used.

Guests still came occasionally although social life was already gradually dying away. Soon in fact no one could any longer say with certainty whether a so-called colleague had not in the meantime changed into a denunciator. For my husband, with his open disposition, his trustfulness, and warmth, the intrusion of this freezing element into personal friendships and professional relationships was a sore trial. Dietrich's manifest support was all the more precious to us on that account. Again and again he opened a new horizon to us which was not so dark, although he fully understood our dilemma and saw all the problems involved. He actually lived what he later came to express in the following terms: 'We are not Christ, but if we wish to be Christians then this means that we must achieve a share in the breadth of Christ's own heart by taking responsible action, action in which, in all freedom, we seize upon the hour and expose ourselves to danger.... To wait inactive and to look on numbly are not Christian attitudes. What summons Christians to action and to compassion is not primarily what they experience in their own bodies but what is experienced in the bodies of their brothers for whose sake Christ has suffered.'

With regard to his work in the Confessing Church and his activities in the struggle of the Church I may refer to the outstanding biography of his friend, Eberhard Bethge, *Dietrich Bonhoeffer, Theologian—Christian—Contemporary*, in which all this is treated of *in extenso*. Already in the first years of the Church's struggle Dietrich told us much of what moved him to action. My mother in Berlin also saw to it that he kept her precisely informed. She took an extraordinary interest in questions of Church politics and Dietrich was glad to discuss very many matters with her.

In 1937 we met Dietrich once more at my parents' home. He had just gone to bed with a most unpleasant attack of influenza. My husband, who sat beside his bed, was having a conversation with him when Dietrich suddenly said to him, 'You and I will not live long lives'. After we had left Germany we met Dietrich again in London in March 1939.

When the danger that Hitler would put his plans for war into action became acute Dietrich, who was in London at the time, sought out Professor Niebuhr who had come from New York and was then spending his European holidays at Bexhill. Gert accompanied Dietrich on his visit to him. Dietrich told Niebuhr the information he had received about the probable outbreak of war in the autumn, and of the fact that the Council of the Brethren had now urged him if at all possible to go to the United States. He also told him that he did not wish to support Hitler's war. Dietrich said that he would like to give some lectures in the States in the summer. Professor Niebuhr immediately telephoned to try to arrange an invitation for him to give a course of lectures during the summer term at the Union Theological Seminary. The answer came in May in the affirmative. Dietrich was also thinking of some post in a parish church, since he did not regard an exclusively academic life as legitimate. On the 7th June Dietrich travelled to New York but by the 13th July he had already returned and stayed two weeks longer with us in London before returning to Germany. His solicitude for his young theologians, as also for those who were being oppressed in Germany, occupied the forefront of his mind to such an extent that his own personal interests were completely secondary. Dietrich's considerations in 1939 which led to the decision to return once more to Germany from the security of America have been described by Reinhold Niebuhr as 'among the finest expressions of Christian martyrdom'. Prior to his return from America Dietrich wrote once more to Niebuhr, who had in fact been the means of obtaining the invitation for him, in the following terms:

'I would have no right to take part in the restoration of Christian life in Germany after the war if I did not share with my nation the trials of this present time. Christians in Germany will find themselves faced with the terrible alternative of whether to desire the defeat of their nation in order that Christian civilization may survive or to desire the victory of their nation and thereby the destruction of our civilization. I know which of these alternatives I must choose, but I cannot make this choice in security.'

Dietrich was no saint. But Christ was 'his life and therefore his conscience too'.

An idea which may be applied to Dietrich is that expressed in these words of Martin Buber, 'A quality proper to a great character is that he acts with his entire being. And this means that it is characteristic of him in particular to react to every situation that demands his active engagement as a man in accordance with the uniqueness of that situation.... By a great character I mean one who, through his actions and attitude, fulfils the claims which the situation makes upon him from a profound readiness to take the responsibility of his own life, and that, too, in such a way that the unity of his nature in its readiness to take this responsibility is manifested in the fact that in his actions his whole being is committed and engaged'.

The stages described in E. Bethge's biography, *Dietrich Bonhoeffer, Theologian-Christian-Contemporary*, are to be understood not as separate states following one upon another in a chronological sequence, as though Dietrich left the Christian behind him once he became a Contemporary, but rather in the sense that every advance to a fresh stage in life subsumed the preceding ones within itself. As a man of our own times he 'lived Christianity' and became a Christian in a true and effective sense, provided one understands the definition of being a Christian as living for others here in this world, and actually committing one's life to uphold the cause of Christ. At one time Dietrich had come near to being a pacifist. But now he actively engaged himself and became a resistance fighter in the group gathered under Admiral Canaris against the régime of Hitler which weighed down the fatherland with crimes and betrayed it. He wanted to contribute towards a better Germany. Thus he did not even shrink from the idea of a supra-national collaboration and in the summer of 1942 he imparted to the Bishop of Chichester the plans of the resistance movement for a new order in Germany based on law after Hitler had been overthrown. In October 1945 the Bishop of Chichester wrote the following words in *The Contemporary Review*:

'... While Bonhoeffer and I were alone I asked him very privately if he could tell me the names of the chief conspirators. He gave them at once. The important people in the plot were, he said, Colonel-General von Beck, Chief of the General Staff before the Austrian crisis in 1938—he was trusted in the army, a Christian, conservative, and in touch with trade union leaders; Colonel-General Hammerstein, Supreme Commander of the Army when Hitler came to power, older, a convinced Christian; Karl Goerdeler, a former Lord Mayor of Leipzig, and an ex-Reich Commissioner for Price Control, highly esteemed by Civil Service people and the leader on the civil front: Whilhelm Leuschner, President of the United Trade Unions before they were dissolved; and Jakob Kaiser, a Catholic trade union leader. Von Beck and Goerdeler were the principals. If a movement under their leadership were to come up it could, in Bonhoeffer's judgement, be relied upon as trustworthy. There was an organization representing the opposition in every Ministry and offices in all the big towns. And there were Generals, or officers quite near the Generals, in all the commands of the Home Front. He mentioned von Kluge and von Witzleben.

I could see that as he told me these facts he was full of sorrow that things had come to such a pass in Germany, and that action like this was necessary. He said that sometimes he felt, "Oh, we have to be punished".'

On this Eberhard Bethge writes, 'For those who perform such an act there can never be any protection. They must venture upon it stripped of all supports and all defences; all those supports which a man otherwise finds in the fact that he is acting under orders, or that his action is approved of, or that he has public opinion behind him.... A nation is basically poor if it is only willing to include in its annals those acts which have been crowned with success'.

We show ourselves to be men of conscience when, in embarking upon a course of action, we refuse to be swayed by our chances of success. We are able to hope because the Cross of Christ at Golgotha stands before us, too, as a symbol of that success which is rooted in failure. After the attempt of the 20th July had miscarried, Dietrich wrote from the prison cell in Tegel in which he had already been held captive in isolation for some three months:

'In these last years I have learnt more and more to recognize and to understand the fact that Christianity belongs profoundly to this present world. The Christian is not a *homo religiosus* but a man in the absolute sense as Jesus was man. The "this-wordliness" of which I speak is not the flat banal worldliness of the enlightened, the busy, the comfortably off or the lascivious, but rather that deep "this-worldliness" which is full of discipline and in which there is an ever-present recognition of death and resurrection. It is this kind of "this-worldliness" that I mean. . . . Today and right down to this present hour I see and experience the fact that we only learn to believe in the full "this-worldliness" of life when we have utterly renounced the aim of making anything of ourselves whether it be a saint or a repentant sinner, a churchman, a figure endowed with so-called priestly qualities, a just man or an unjust one, a sick man or a healthy one. And this is what I call "this-worldliness", namely living in the midst of all those tasks, questions, successes and failures, experiences and bewilderments which come to us. Then we throw ourselves utterly into the arms of God. Then our deepest thoughts are directed not to our own suffering but to the suffering of God in the world. Then we watch with Christ in Gethsemane, and I think that that is faith, that is *metanoia*, and it is in this way that one becomes a man, a Christian.'

In January 1943 Dietrich became engaged to Maria von Wedemeyer, a daughter of the owner of Pätzig, an estate in the Neumark, and his wife, née von Kleist-Retzow. The engagement was kept secret. Unfortunately I only met Maria in 1947 at Göttingen after our return. She was studying mathematics there. She impressed me as being a particularly beautiful and warm-hearted young girl, indefatigable, able and energetic.

On the 5th April 1943 Dietrich was arrested together with our brother-in-law, Hans von Dohnanyi. Dietrich was sent to Tegel Military Prison and put in solitary confinement. From this period we have letters to his parents and his friend, Eberhard Bethge. The letters and writings which issued from his cell have been collected in the book entitled *Letters and Papers from Prison*. A warder who was well-disposed towards him smuggled them out.

Dietrich knew how to establish human contact with some of his warders. One even wanted to help him to escape. This was frustrated by the arrest of our brother, Klaus, for Dietrich feared that reprisals would be taken against those related to him, who were already in great danger. Today we know what Dietrich came to mean to many of his fellow prisoners. He spent the time in Tegel in concentrated work on his *Ethics* and in the struggle against his accusers. He wrote to his friend with firm conviction that it was precisely 'the enduring of such an extreme situation, with all the problems it entails, that is my task'.

It was his effort constantly to allay our parents' anxiety that gave his letters their confident tone. He was never sorry for himself and in his imprisonment at Tegel and in the cellars of the S.S. prison in Prinz-Albrecht-Strasse, in the concentration camp at Buchenwald and even on the way to the liquidation centre of the camp at Flossenbürg, the effect he had upon his fellow prisoners was in accordance with that verse of Tersteegen which he so much liked to sing: 'If a weaker man should fall the stronger man should stand by him. We must help and sustain all, and spread love and peace.'

In the early hours of the 9th April 1945 Dietrich was hanged by the Gestapo at Flossenbürg. Admiral Canaris, Major-General Oster, Dr Sack, the advocate Strünck and Captain Gehre were executed together with him.

'Rebellion against tyrants is obedience to God', as Thomas Jefferson had already said.

Dietrich bore witness with his life to what he set down in writing whilst in prison:

'To do and to dare not what pleases one but what is right;
not to stay hovering in the realm of the merely possible, but
boldly to commit oneself to the actual—freedom consists
not in taking refuge in ideas but is to be found in deeds alone.
Go forth from anxious waverings into the tempest of events,
sustained only by God's command and your own faith, and
freedom will receive your spirit triumphantly.'

9

Susanne

My youngest sister, Susi, was born in 1909, entering the world three and a half years after us twins, and we soon found ourselves having to give her a place in our games. She was an extremely vivacious and energetic small person with black hair and dark eyes. She played with incredible intensity, turned everything upside down, and was reluctant to tidy up. Even during her childhood I can see so many of those qualities develop in her which she later exhibited in her life as a pastor's wife. At four years old she divided one square of chocolate from a bar into seven pieces, so that the last of those waiting to receive a crumb received instead only her little thumb stuck into his mouth. She soon won friends of her own among the little girls that she knew.

During her childhood her birthday, which was generally celebrated in our country home during the holidays, set half the village in motion. Not less than fifty little boys and girls who were her friends would take part. My parents were strongly in favour of us playing with the village children but first all the children were given water, soap, and a towel to wash their hands before going on to the birthday chocolate, the whipping tops, and the games. Susi still has such large gatherings when she invites members of the congregation to highly imaginative and 'un-pastoral' parties.

She treated school as of secondary importance, a fact which was later reflected in her reports. At that time only her encounters with the other children were important to her. There were times in which she felt hurt and full of the world's sorrows, feeling that people did not understand her or appreciate her enough. But her pronounced gift for making contact with people always helped her to recover.

At twenty-one she married Pastor Walter Dress, then a lecturer in Church history and a friend of Dietrich's student days. He, too, had his licence to teach at the University of Berlin withdrawn by the National Socialists. Susi gave shelter and concealment to several Jews and supplied them with food and clothing. She receives acknowledgement for this even today. Apart from a brief period at Dorpat, she has lived in Berlin ever since she was three years old and still lives there today, and, moreover, is unwilling ever to leave Berlin. She has two sons of whom one is today a professor of mathematics and the other is a musician living in England. She has an astonishing energy for work, is always active on behalf of others, and sought after by those who have problems and need help. In the post-war years she was tireless in caring for the welfare of refugees. As soon as she had coped with her duties in one field she would discover another field where she was needed. She almost always has solutions for disasters, and is a pastor's wife in the true sense, not one who makes a martyr of herself but a cheerful, enterprising wife, who, with her resolution, energy, and vitality, carries many along with her.

PART TWO

REMINISCENCES OF
THE PERIOD FROM 1924 TO 1938

10

Marriage

In the year 1924 I became engaged to Gerhard Leibholz. At that time it was not yet the custom in the world to which we belonged to go out alone with a young man prior to one's engagement. We saw each other at a certain distance and occasionally might have some conversation when friends of our brothers came to the house. For the most part, however, the young men were engaged in their work and in discussions with their men friends in their rooms where, as a girl, one did not join them. I also remember Mama saying to my sixteen-year-old sister, Christel, 'Another thing, child, if Hans again wants to put flowers out as a surprise for you he must not simply bring them into your room. That is not done. There might actually be stockings or clothes belonging to you lying about. He must give them to you through Fräulein Emma'.

The way in which we came to converse and to know one another was rather through the invitations and the balls which my parents often gave, on walks and excursions in which we, our brothers, their men friends and our girl friends, were brought together. Even with this, right up to the time at which we became engaged we still called one another 'Fräulein Bonhoeffer' and 'Herr Leibholz'. After the engagement had been announced we could go for walks alone together or to the theatre or to concerts. But even then it would have been inconceivable to travel anywhere alone together.

My husband, Gerhard Leibholz, was descended on his mother's side from a family of industrialists from Baden. He grew up in very comfortable circumstances. Unfortunately I never came to know my husband's mother. She must have been tall and stately, evidently she was naive and very amiable. She had three sons. Unfortunately her health was not altogether sound, and during the influenza epidemic of 1922, to which so many fell victim, she, too, could not be saved. She had a particularly close relationship with my husband, and he felt her loss infinitely hard to bear.

His father's side of the family came from Bärwalde in Pomerania. Gert's father had textile factories in Lichtenberg near Berlin and in Forst, later, too, in Sommerfeld. He was first a city councillor and then an alderman of Berlin, Wilmersdorf and he loved to occupy himself with civic affairs. He also instituted school meals at his own cost. He lived in his house in the Kurfürstendamm in Berlin and at a later stage acquired a fine and very large house in the Grunewald by the Königssee. My father-in-law, William Leibholz, was a tall, large man, very upright in his bearing and always very well groomed. He had a great deal of common sense and business acumen, though in other matters he was somewhat less sophisticated. He was a warmhearted, solicitous father, father-in-law and grandfather, and wise enough to allow each of his sons to follow the profession each recognized as right for himself. He told me a story of my husband's childhood which had touched him. At three years old Gert was lost in the zoological gardens. The panic-stricken nursemaid had the alarm bell rung for him. His brothers shouted his name at the top of their voices. And all the time Gert (at home he was only called 'Simple Simon', his eldest brother being extremely intelligent) was making his way home with total self-reliance. Right through the zoological garden he steered his course purposefully towards his family home, at that time in the Joachimsthaler Strasse. He still recalls, even today, the astonished questions of some of the passers-by: 'Hallo, little one, where do you want to go? Where is your Mummy?' He went on, singing softly to himself, and finally stumped up the steps, actually reached up to the bell, and, when his kind mother sought to take him in her arms he said to her, 'I am not silly, I am clever too'.

At six years old Gert was a militarist. On his seventh birthday he asked for lead soldiers. But once when his good nanny came into the nursery she saw that all his soldiers had been laid out round the table and that Gert had twisted the heads off every one of them, laying them down beside their original owners. When his shocked nurse asked, 'Gert, what have you been doing?' he answered, 'Well Nanny, after all it is Remembrance Sunday for the dead!' Unfortunately Gert can no longer recall what was going on in his head at that time. Soon afterwards he was very much vexed at what he had done, and tried to stick the heads back on with various kinds of glue, but quite unsuccessfully. Earlier he had given the lead soldiers the names of great generals, and he thought that this made it impossible for him to throw them away. Together with his brothers, therefore, Gert devised a very militarist solution to the problem by putting the beheaded soldiers in little boxes together with flowers. Then every time Gert went for a walk in the Grunewald he buried one of these little boxes and laid out a warriors' cemetery which he visited again and again.

Gert says that right up to his fifteenth year he was firmly convinced that all men were good. All relatives were particularly good, but still as a general principle: men were good. On one occasion when his mother made a critical remark about one of their relatives he had to come down from the clouds, was extremely upset, and thereafter began for the first time to have some idea that those about him could, perhaps, not be good.

During the confirmation classes which he attended Gert made friends with Hans von Dohnanyi, and later he was a friend and fellow student of my brother Klaus. My parents found Gert particularly likeable as an individual. His open nature, his intelligence and intellectual interests went hand in hand with a certain naiveté; and a further quality which they particularly valued was his unpretentiousness. On one occasion I heard my father saying to my brothers, 'Of all these young people of yours who now come so often to the house I really like talking to young Leibholz best of all. He is both intelligent and unpretentious'.

Nevertheless my parents were far from enthusiastic when I told them that we had become engaged. Gert was only twenty-two while I was eighteen. 'Whatever have you been getting up to?' asked my father, and my mother remarked, 'Oh child, you could have had a much easier time! Now things will be difficult for you. It is doubtful whether Gert will advance as far in his profession as he deserves, and that is an experience which it is very sad for a wife to have to watch. See how long Papa has been trying to obtain a professorship for Herr X. Like Gert, he, too, is of Jewish descent. In all these years it has been simply impossible to achieve it. And yet he is outstandingly able. In any case you are still terribly young. . . .'

In short we still had to wait for our marriage. My father did not allow his daughters to get married under twenty years of age. The time of the engagement should be used for the purpose of coming to know one another better. In the course of our engagement my husband wrote his second book on *Equality Before the Law*. At that time his first book, *Fichte and the Idea of Democracy*, with which he had gained his doctorate of philosophy at the age of nineteen, had already been published. The thesis on 'Equality' for his doctorate in law appeared in 1925. In this he concerned himself with a problem which was to be the subject of passionate discussion all during the latter part of the twenties and right up to the onset of National Socialism. It provided the constitutional lawyers of the time with their most significant subject for debate, namely the 'omnipotence' of the lawgiver. Even after the Second World War the main question raised in this book still played a notable part in the discussion of constitutional law. Gert had the satisfaction that the Federal Constitutional Court at which he became a judge in 1951 accepted his views as expressed in his book in 1925 in exactly the same wording in a famous decision in 1951. Recently the book itself has once more been reprinted, unaltered in all essentials after thirty-four years. Since then the question as to whether a statute law, a government or administrative act are in accordance with the principle of equality before the law is one of the most hotly argued subjects with which the court has to deal again and again.

In 1926 when we were married I had not yet completed any course of professional training. I had been attending an art school to pursue my special bent for drawing while at twenty-four my husband had already achieved his two doctorates and his second law degree of *Assessor*. But he was only earning 390 Reichsmarks and we would not have been able to find enough to live on (our flat of four and a half rooms alone had already cost 6,000 Reichsmarks in key money apart from the rent of 225 Reichsmarks a month) if Gert's father had not made some contribution towards this. The same picture was to be found in the recent marriages of my three sisters. My parents had to give them financial help. They did not wish us to marry without being in a position to employ a servant.

On the 31st March 1926 Gert took his second law examination and on the 6th April we celebrated our wedding amid a large circle of guests and set off for Lugano.

At that time the celebration of a marriage of any size lasted almost three days. The day before our eve-of-wedding party was dominated by the arrival of our wedding guests and the morning of this day was already full of joyful anticipation as well as being taken up with the final preparations and rehearsals, though as the bridal couple we were not burdened with this. For us everything had to remain a surprise.

At the eve-of-wedding party, at six o'clock in the evening, about sixty excited guests whom we had invited from all generations arrived in their party clothes. The gentlemen wore evening dress and the ladies ball dresses. After greeting their hosts everyone sat down and Barbara Kempner (née Hildebrandt) and Frau von Dohnanyi, the pianist, played Beethoven's 'Spring Sonata', the piece I had asked for. Then after an interval for conversation my younger sister and my brother Dietrich entertained us with an early nineteenth-century song and dance by Max Bierbaum entitled *Ringel-Reihe-Rosenkranz, ich tanz mit meiner Frau*. This was charming and earned great applause. In the meantime, the grand buffet had been set up and we had dinner. After the meal two golden chairs decorated with garlands were placed in the centre of the floor and we had to sit on them. Now the song 'We bind for you the maiden's crown' rang out from the piano as the door opened and the bridesmaids danced in with garlands in their hair. They bore a green garland bound with silken ribbons of violet and blue. With it they formed a circle round us and danced about us singing the 'We bind for you the maiden's crown' taking turns to recite the verses from the *Freischütz*. The verse 'Lavender, myrtle and thyme, that's what grows in our garden, How long till a suitor comes? I can hardly wait,' occasioned great enjoyment.

The bridesmaids laid the green garland decked with ribbons at our feet and my youngest sister now stepped forward with a garland of red roses in her hand. She recited some verses which my grandmother had written long before for my mother's eve-of-marriage party and laid the garland of roses upon my head.

My brothers and sisters and my friends had composed a very witty *Hobelbank* (literally 'joiner's bench') as it was called, and this was sung by my brothers to tunes from the opera. At the same time, pictures which had been specially painted to go with this were shown. At that time we did not yet have any bands or radios to dance by, but we did have a very good pianist who played dance music for us, and he began with a waltz by Strauss. From time to time my brother-in-law, Rüdiger Schleicher, picked up his violin, too, giving even more of a swing to the music. Gert and I opened the dance. Then my parents danced a waltz alone while the guests stood round applauding. After that my father-in-law asked me to dance with him and when that was over the whole company finally took the floor. All at once from the well of the stairs a great hubbub broke out of rattling and clattering and the noise of breaking crockery. Cups, dishes, glasses, plates ... Anna, our old cook, was dashing them vehemently to the floor and the maids were helping her. The more the fragments, the greater the luck! It seemed that the clatter would never end until finally my mother had to signal to them to stop. The eve-of-wedding party ended shortly before midnight.

On the morning of our wedding day, a little before seven o'clock, I heard the hasty tiptoeing of many feet outside my bedroom door, and finally a chorus of voices breaking out in song. Loud and solemn the hymn rang out, 'Praise the Lord, the mighty king of glory'. There could be no mistaking the singing of Gert, the strong voice of my mother and those of my brothers and sisters, my relations by marriage, and friends of the family. After that my mother visited me briefly in my room. My father-in-law and my brothers-in-law were expected at breakfast and a festival table had been laid. This hour of the morning was solemn but festive. After breakfast we all went into the drawing room where Dietrich played us Edward Grieg's *Hochzeitstag auf Trollhagen*. Gert and I then sat side by side on a sofa and all our relations found themselves places round about while my sister Christel stepped forward with my bridal wreath on a white silken cushion and recited to me the wedding poem which my grandmother had also composed:

Sister, on your wedding day
I bring to you as bride
The wreath of your dedication.
My heart is deeply moved,
For today the garland of myrtle,
Symbol of purity and faithfulness,
Is lying in your hands.
I feel my heart beating at one with yours,
I am at one with you in the thoughts of your heart.
I pray God that he may guide your life henceforward
Into a blessed course.
Indeed where love unites two hearts,
There will the path of life be bright and easy.
One finds courage and joy in the other,
One gives consolation and help to the other.
In union with God, therefore,
Advance into your new life.
The myrtle fades but love endures for ever.
And if I must let you depart from me,
May God bless you, your fortune and your house.
When soon the marriage bells ring out
That old song of faithfulness to death,
Then believe that you are encompassed by our good wishes
Gathered up in the prayer, 'Go forth with God!'

It was only with difficulty that Christel could be persuaded to perform, and she had to summon up all her resolution to give this recital. But traditionally it fell to her, and now she recited the verses quite simply, and so it went off well. Nor did these verses lay any claim at the time to be the product of high artistic inspiration. They were handed down because they had once expressed my grandmother's thoughts for the happy life she wished our mother, and they were dear to our mother's heart; also because, after all, these wishes must surely always remain the same, regardless of whether the tastes of a particular epoch express them in a different form.

By this time the morning was over and it was time to go to

the registry office. My father and father-in-law accompanied us as witnesses to the marriage. We went on foot and my father enjoyed the walk. It was a sunny but still cool April day. When we returned home my mother greeted me and Gert with a kiss. With us it was only on very special occasions that we received kisses from our parents. I can positively count the number of times that this happened.

Upstairs in front of my mother's dressing-table our old hair-dresser was waiting. Later he had to put on my garland and veil in accordance with instructions from Mama. At last everything had been arranged. I had put on the bridal dress with my sisters and the maids bustling round and my aunt, too, giving her advice as to how the veil would hang best, when suddenly the bridal wreath was missing! There was a hasty search on all sides until it was found hanging from my aunt's lace shawl! Finally, when they were satisfied with me, I cautiously made my way down the stairs accompanied by my 'retinue' and saw my husband and my father already waiting below. In the meantime Gert, too, had put on his tail coat, and now he gave me my wedding bouquet. The bridesmaids and best man had now assembled in their wedding clothes.

The bridal carriage had driven up to the garden door and also the carriages for the members of the family and the wedding guests. We got into the wedding coach, which had been decked out with white silk and was drawn by two pretty white horses, while our relations and guests drove on before us to the Grune-wald church so as to be able to be in their places and receive us there before the wedding procession. Soon after we arrived Pastor Priebe appeared, the same pastor who had confirmed both of us. Gert and I had previously visited Pastor Priebe again, and I had chosen on behalf of us both that verse which runs: 'Create in me a clean heart, O God; and renew a right spirit within me. Restore unto me the joy of thy salvation and uphold me with thy free spirit'. Pastor Priebe was not wholly in agreement with my choice and remarked that he had never yet preached on this text at a wedding. But finally he consented to do so. We sang 'God is present' and 'Jesus go before us'. In addition to these hymns we, of course, had 'Where thou goest, there will I go too'.

By three o'clock we had all re-assembled back at the house where the wedding table all decked with flowers was waiting for us. My father, my brother Dietrich, a cousin, friends and Pastor Priebe made speeches. Some of the other guests, too, said a few words and everyone drank our healths.

Even after Gert and I had already set out late that afternoon in the direction of Lugano the marriage guests still remained together into the late evening. On the following morning the young people met again to take a cheerful walk in the Grunewald. This concluded the wedding celebrations.

During the first years of our marriage, from 1926-9, my husband and I continued to live in Berlin and our circle of friends and relations increased. On the 30th June 1927 our first child was born to us, a little girl. Marianne was christened in my parents' house, and this again was a wonderful family festival. My twin brother, Dietrich, was godfather.

This meant that our flat was already too small, and I still remember how our elderly but energetic nanny, who came from East Prussia, hung baby clothes all over the balcony where Gert had always liked to work. And when he asked whether somewhere else could not be found for this she tartly replied, 'Herr Doctor, he who says A must also say B!' It was only after a prolonged discussion which I had with her about which came first, the baby clothes or a suitable place for the head of the family to work, that she condescended to relegate the baby clothes to second place.

My husband was now a judge of the district court but soon a post as *Referent* in the Institute for Foreign Public Law and International Law was offered him. He took over the Italian section. His work in this department stimulated him to bring out another book in 1928 entitled *On the Problems of Fascist Constitutional Law*. He also gave his inaugural lecture on this subject at the university. Gert took his lecturer's examination (Habilitation) in Berlin in 1928.

11

The first years of
professional life at Greifswald

In 1929 my husband obtained his first professorship. He was offered the chair of Constitutional Law at the University of Greifswald. At that time he was just twenty-eight, and it meant that we had to leave Berlin, where we had grown up and where our family homes were situated. But it was the beginning of his academic career and there was never any question as to whether he should accept the appointment. I can still vividly remember the journey to Pomerania. It led through the stations of Pasewalk and Anklam, where no living soul was to be seen on the platform and where we were surrounded by an almost uncanny stillness.

The little town of Greifswald made a very sleepy impression on us as we drove from the station to the Preussenhof hotel. Here we were touched to find that the host had reserved the 'Princes' room for us. In the centre of the parlour at this hotel stood a large round table at which at times the dignitaries of the town used to gather. Later we often had meals with our colleagues at this table. At little individual tables sat a few taciturn individuals with glasses of spirits beside them. Outside the snow was falling, while inside it was excessively warm and incredibly still and restful. One hardly dared to break the silence. We felt ourselves under a spell. After a good meal of roast goose and a glass of spirits we tramped on through the snowy streets of the old 'Gryps'. Before us lay the fine market-place with its gothic outlines, while behind it rose the massive pile of the 'Dicke Marie', the brick-built gothic church.

We moved into a small, recently built house with a garden at the end of the town where the road led to the old ruins of the monastery of Eldena and further on to the Bodden where one could swim. From the sea a very fresh, biting wind was always blowing, but it made us hardy and we had very little sickness while we were living here.

The best point was that we were so near to the open fields. When we stepped out of doors after meals they lay sun-drenched and undulating before us, and at such times we used to saunter along the narrow paths and enjoy the wind and the scent of the corn while I picked myself many a bunch of poppies and cornflowers.

In the midst of this summer joy, a letter arrived from Dietrich's study in Berlin:

Berlin   29th June 1930

Dear Sabine, dear Gert,

The thought of little Marianne's birthday tomorrow reminds me once more of those pleasant days which I was recently able to spend with you. I would gladly have travelled up with your father-in-law in order to see you again and take part in your celebrations of this day. As it is, please accept my heartfelt greetings and so many good wishes. For on the first few birthdays one really thinks more of the parents who are certainly in a better position to value good wishes than the actual person concerned. But just the same please give lots of love from me to Marianne as well. I wanted so much to send her something more but I never found time for it and I believe she will not hold it against me. I have another fourteen days' work to do and then, if all goes well with everything, that is with the second examination and the trial lecture, I shall have finished. Although in theory I had intended to do hardly any special work for the examination, I cannot keep to this resolve and thus the entire day is taken up and always passes quickly. Yesterday we had company. Triepel has so much to say and Uncle Rudi apparently told so many improper jokes that the conversation was very lively. As I write I am listening to the Weigerts' dance music through my open window. Solitary

couples are walking in the garden—just as in the old days!—
and I am longing for nothing more than to join in the dancing.
Mama is fairly fully occupied with Susi. If only we could have
some quiet in the house! There is no lack of this at your
home, and I know you can appreciate how wonderful that
it. Farewell, give my love to Marianne, with many heartfelt
wishes, and thinking of you tomorrow,

Yours, Dietrich

In December 1930 our second daughter, Christiane, was born
to us. My mother had already sent me an experienced nanny,
but she still wanted to be ready at call to come to Greifswald
with my father in the car and to bring along the midwife who
had previously attended me and whom she trusted. Dietrich, too,
was thinking of me and wrote to me from New York:

New York   7th November 1930

Dear Sabine,

I was so glad to have your letter. Very many thanks for it.
It is always so pleasant when something from Germany comes
through the letter-box in the morning. You will already be
preparing for the little brother or sister, you believe at the
beginning of December. But in any case even at this stage I
am thinking of you several times a day from across the water
with many good wishes. Of course you will let me know at
once? Here it has become rather wintry, and though it is
not thirty-five degrees below zero, as your newspaper says,
still it is about thirty-five degrees fahrenheit, that is about zero
with us. The sky is a splendid blue, though the wind is rough.
Thus it is no time to go out; in any case I would hardly
have time to do so. I now constantly find myself having to
give talks and addresses and on the most varied occasions.
The day after tomorrow I have to preach in English and next
week I have to give a talk to a thousand schoolchildren about
Germany. One has a fairly strong feeling here of being considered
the expert, and in fact that isn't altogether pleasant. But still life
in the Seminary is really agreeable and useful. A whole year

has passed and I have still not become acquainted with all three hundred of the members. The only thing is that, for the most part, not much emerges from the discussions. One always has the feeling that one is talking to sixth-form boys. There are, of course, a few who are different, one still finds interesting people, especially among the coloured students and those from Eastern Asia, and in fact the opportunities here are particularly favourable for coming to know people from every conceivable country. Here in the Seminary there are more than forty foreigners. Opposite us stands the 'International House for Students' and a few evenings ago we took part in a gathering which included ninety-seven different nationalities. At the end of November there is a week's holiday at the seminary, when I will travel to Washington with one of the coloured students who is here. I must close because I have accepted an invitation. I wish you every conceivable happiness for the next few weeks. My heartfelt good wishes to you, Gert, and to Marianne.

Yours, Dietrich

When Gert telephoned my parents in the morning they set out in the car with the midwife, but on the way they had a breakdown and my poor mother was in despair. It was only in the late afternoon that they arrived. Papa immediately pulled out his watch in order to time the labour pains and smilingly remarked, 'You still have a little while to go', which at that moment I did not much appreciate. But I was now completely calm because he was there, and my father was right! It was only after midnight that Christiane entered the world. The midwife's cry of 'a little girl' still rings in my ears even today. She was from southern Germany and remarked, 'This one will be a beauty'. And in fact our Christiane already seemed pretty to us.

In my room my parents, together with Gert, the gynaecologist, the midwife and the nurse, drank a glass of champagne to the health of Christiane and myself. A telegram was sent straightaway to Dietrich in America, where he was already expecting it. Dietrich's telegram of congratulations arrived surprisingly quickly, and a little later a long letter came from him full of kindness. On a journey to Florida with a theological student he sent me a picture postcard:

St Augusta   15th December 1930

Dear Sabine,

How much I should like to put a branch of this sort (together with the oranges) in your room. Then you would quickly get well merely from looking at it. As it is you will simply have to gather from the picture how splendid it is that I can see all this here actually in the flesh. I have travelled from the winter in New York right into the midst of summer. Today I have been lying in the sun for a few hours in a palm grove. It is fantastically beautiful. All best wishes. What a pity that we cannot share this kind of experience together. Tomorrow we are going still further south. Loving good wishes.

Yours, Dietrich

In his professional work Gert was not overburdened. He enjoyed the lectures and liked the students in his seminars. He had time for research and it was a pleasant winter. At that time Gert gave me a present of a very handsome and comfortable chair which he put next to his desk. Here he wanted me to sit with him with a book or some needlework. It was something that he liked and I, too, found it pleasant even though I often had to keep an eye open because our daughters were still small and needed much care from me, the nursemaid being very young. One by one we became personally acquainted with our colleagues at Greifswald, first those belonging to our own faculty and then those from the faculties of theology and medicine together with their wives. The atmosphere at the university was pleasant and harmonious.

There were many excursions to the Bodden. We could already sense its proximity from the smell of fish in the old bus by which the fishwives journeyed to and from Greifswald with their baskets. Even the eggs often tasted of fish. We liked to eat 'eel in a green sauce' with our colleagues and their wives in the little fishing village of Gristow. I remember one colleague was evidently particularly keen on his eel, and he regarded the one general order to bring us 'eels in a green sauce' as not being very advantageous to himself. He called out to the waiter, 'Please bring all the eels on separate dishes!' We were much amused at this.

As neighbours, we had living on the left of us Dr Hürthle of the medical faculty, whose father had been a colleague of my father at Breslau and whom therefore I already knew, while on the right lived Kneser, the mathematician, with his sensible and pleasant wife. His father, too, was a professor at Breslau and had been a close friend of the Bonhoeffer family. Among the theologians we met Jeremias, who, like my husband, soon afterwards took up an appointment at Göttingen. We also met the wise and understanding Catholic priest, Fr Wachsmann, and highly esteemed him. At that time he looked after the Polish land workers who used to come over to do the field work in the summer and had many difficulties. Later, after the 20th July 1944, this priest was to pay with his life for the part he played in the resistance to Hitler. A son of the painter Steinhausen who was professor of medicine had his father's fine pictures still hanging in his house and he gave me his father's charming picture-book *Cinderella*, as a present for our daughters. There were many, many new acquaintances. In the course of our life we have often looked back to some of these with great pleasure.

Our children were developing well under the great broad sky which was constantly changing. It was a joy to look at the clouds with them when we went for walks along the Ryck. But unfortunately we were already beginning to feel something of the political storm that was blowing up. There were nearly four and a half million unemployed. In the Reichstag election in September 1930 the N.S.D.A.P. (National Socialist German Workers' Party) increased their mandate from twelve to more than a hundred. In Pomerania even as early as 1930-1 one could already come across many indications of the direction in which politics were moving. For instance, on one occasion when we were going to visit one of our acquaintances we saw on entering the garden door a man raking up the leaves who was dressed in a uniform which was unfamiliar to us and wearing jackboots. A little flaxen-haired boy, the youngest son of our acquaintance, jumped out to meet us.

I asked, 'Who is this man then? Has he not got a tropical uniform on?'

Grinning broadly and laughing, the boy replied, 'Do you not know what an S.A. man is?'

I did not know—not yet.

Emboldened by my ignorance he asked, 'Do you know the Horst-Wessel song?'

No, I did not know it—not yet.

Accordingly, with a lisping intonation, for just then he was in the process of losing his first teeth and a broad gap could be seen in his upper set, he sang us all the verses of that dreadful song.

We found ourselves involved in another very nasty situation in the market-place at Stralsund through the actions of an S.A. group. My father-in-law had visited us in Greifswald and had gone on an excursion with us and his chauffeur in his big 'Horch' car. He hardly ever had time for this and we had all looked forward to the trip to Stralsund. In the market-place, the S.A. pressed insolently against the windows and jostled against the car which at that time was travelling very slowly. Some louts banged on the windows and took up a pretty threatening attitude of which my father-in-law was the object. Very quickly I took our four-year-old Marianne, who at that time was flaxen-haired and blue-eyed, from my lap and put her on her grandfather's knee. This saved the situation and we were able to drive on undisturbed. But the shock remained and we could see black clouds ahead.

All this time Dietrich had still been in the United States and he wrote to me about his plans for the future as follows:

New York   21st January 1931

Dear Sabine,

It is a pity that just now the ships are leaving at such awkward times. Tomorrow there is one that will actually be in Germany on the 28th while the next one only leaves on the next 28th. This would mean that you would only receive your letter on the 6th February, hence you will now be getting your birthday letter at a time when perhaps you are not really thinking of your birthday at all. Unfortunately I have not yet been able to get what I wanted for you as a present, because of influenza I couldn't go into the city. I hope I can send my present by the next ship if it can be sent at all. But please don't get too excited, it really isn't anything special! It strikes me as very odd that we are actually already twenty-five. But strangely I find it more difficult to imagine in your case than in mine. For myself I have simply been able gradually to come to terms with it, but it is still always as a twenty-year-old that you figure in my subconscious thoughts, probably because since we were that age we have no longer lived together. And for all this I cannot really beguile myself into forgetting that you already have quite different achievements to look back to than I. If I had been married for five years, and had two children and a house of my own like you, then I would feel I was fully justified in being twenty-five.

This coming year will in fact be another especially good one for you all now that you again have a very small person in the house. To it and to you I send my very best wishes that you may spend this year in the same quiet and peaceable circumstances as you have had up to now in your pretty little house, which for so long I have been wanting to see again. I am eager to see Marianne once more in a few months and still more little Christiane, who is supposed to look so much like me.

I am sure you will have a lovely birthday celebration. How I shall spend the day I do not quite know yet. Some people here have heard that it is my birthday and demand a birthday party which, if it takes place, I would hold at the house of one of the married students. But perhaps, too, I will find a good play to go to. Unfortunately on this occasion I cannot even drink your health in a glass of wine. The great laws of state prohibit this. It's a terrible nonsense, this prohibition which is imposed though no one believes in it.

Just now we are having the holiday between semesters and I have much time to look to outstanding matters which up to now I have neglected, especially certain visits to make and many books to read. At present I am reading a great deal of negro literature, part of which is really very interesting. Apart from this, I am making a systematic study of American philosophy with one of the professors here.

The political situation in Germany is much talked of here and, moreover, with very great sympathy, especially in academic circles. A professor of economy from the University of Columbia remarked to me that he had no doubt that America would in the foreseeable future introduce changes which would substantially alter the whole question of reparations. The people here themselves complain a great deal, but this does not make a very convincing impression upon us Europeans. Actually only the unemployed for whom there is no kind of security are in a dreadful position.

My plans for the months after May are still completely uncertain. On the one hand I would like to return straightaway to Germany in order to do some work, but even in that case I would certainly spend four to six weeks in travel first, perhaps through the South and West towards Mexico, but perhaps I may still go right round the world, and this means especially to India if the money extends to it and I find someone to accompany me, and also if I do not find the tug of Germany too strong for me. The most likely thing is that I shall be returning to Germany at the end of June.

I wish you a happy and enjoyable birthday and from my heart every good wish for the coming year. My special love to you, Gert, Marianne and little Christiane,

Yours, Dietrich

In May 1931 Gert was offered an appointment in Göttingen as Professor of Constitutional Law. But this no longer gave us any real pleasure. Gert questioned whether it was now worthwhile making any new beginnings. Nevertheless in October we did move to Göttingen and Gert entered upon his new post there. On the 23rd December Dietrich wrote us the following letter:

Dear Sabine, dear Gert,

When one is writing a Christmas letter the limitations of a typewriter are forcibly brought home to one. But since in any case the letter can only be short these limitations can be put up with on this occasion. Really it is a very great pity that you are not coming. We had all looked forward to it and I even made a bet that you could still be shaken in your decision not to come. Unfortunately I now seem finally to have lost this. What a pity! This means that we shall have no children with us at all, and it will not sound very convincing tomorrow when the family chorus, ranging in age from twenty-five to eighty-nine, sings 'You little children come'.

Well, I wish you an especially happy festival in your very small family circle. How are you going to spend it? Are you having to work out your Christmas customs this year right

5. The twins Dietrich and Sabine aged eight

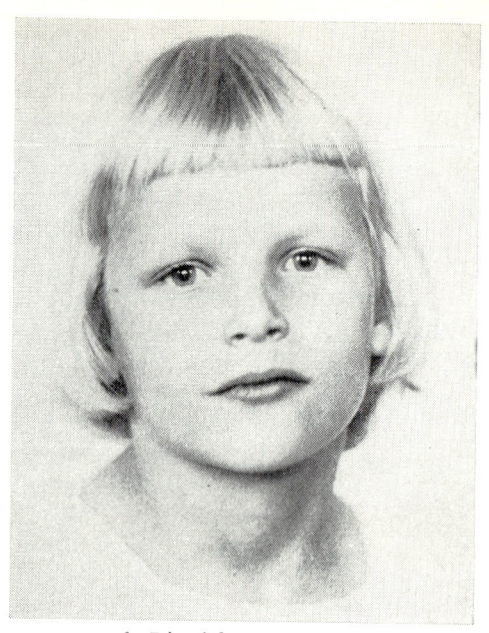

6. Dietrich a) aged six

b) aged eleven   c) aged fifteen

from the beginning? Up to now you always spent Christmas with the family in Berlin, didn't you? We are having real winter weather here but probably, in view of the fact that tomorrow is Christmas, it will change just before then. A year ago I was sitting in the most torrid heat in Cuba. But all that belongs to a different age! A few days ago I went to spend a couple of days in the snow with some of my confirmation candidates. For me, and probably for them too, this was very instructive. This year my interest in Christmas is concentrated very strongly in the direction of these confirmation candidates. And side by side with the work I have to do for my lectures I find the packing of Christmas parcels a change that is very pleasant and that seems to me no less important than that other work.

Tomorrow I shall very often be reaching out to you in my thoughts as surely you will to us. Perhaps we will speak to one another on the telephone. Please give my special love to my godchild. This time she is not getting anything from me (this sounds as though at other times she always gets something, which I hardly think is the case). The true reason is that in these last days I have simply not managed to give adequate thought to Christmas or to prepare myself for it. May all go well with you. Have a happy Christmas and a good new year without too much worrying. After all, this doesn't help very much,

With heartfelt love to you and the children,

Yours, Dietrich

From 1930 onwards Gert foresaw the coming of the Nazis. At that time they already had a third of the votes in the Reichstag. As early as 1932 there was a Union of National Socialist Students at Göttingen and these demanded the right to march in with swastika banners at the opening ceremony of the new semester. However, the Head of the University at the time, Professor Ludwig, forbade this.

D

12

Appointment at Göttingen—
Incipient persecution—Preparations
for emigration

Our house lay far back from the street and had a vine climbing
up the walls between the windows. The house acquired a special
charm at the season when the leaves of this were changing
colour. By the standards of the time it was not a large house,
but downstairs it had a spacious and quiet study for Gert with
plenty of room for our books. Even at that stage we had collected a good library. The view looked out onto our orchard.
Next to this study lay a fine large baroque dining-room with a
round dining-table and a bow-legged breakfast table next to the
garden window. This opened onto the drawing-room in which
stood the grand piano upon which Dietrich often played, as well
as onto a room for me with furniture from the 'Biedermeier'
period. We had a pretty southern veranda where Dietrich liked
to take the sun. The orchard, situated behind the house, was
enchanting, especially when the white beds round the borders
were etched out in sharp relief in the moonlight and also in
blossom time when the morello cherries with their graceful
branches were decked in white blossom. At the same time, however, it entailed more work than I had imagined. Sometimes it
was a burden to cope with all the bushes laden with berries and
the plum, apple and pear trees. When there was a good yield from
all of these we could give them away by the hamperful to
students and acquaintances.

The cellars were filled with the results of our industry,
crammed with home-made jam, bottled fruit and fresh fruit. A
glorious scent rose up to meet one whenever one went down

there. Next to it lay the wine cellar which was filled with bottles of excellent wine by my father-in-law. The garden was a paradise for the children. If the times had not been so difficult we would, of course, have enjoyed it much more.

We still had two years in Göttingen before the devil began to rear his head. Here at Göttingen we could not see very much of the general poverty at this time of economic crisis apart from the queues at the labour offices. Twice a week I prepared lunch for an out-of-work family of six, and also sought about to find clothes for them. Everything else we gathered merely from the newspapers or the radio, for it was not yet the time when the whole world was brought into the house through the medium of television. Of course we already had an inkling of political unrest, but how little idea we then had, for instance, of the United States and the situation of crisis which prevailed there! In these small university towns life was far too circumscribed, and most of the professors were far too out of touch with the world, each living in his own special branch of learning. Admittedly those engaged in the field of natural science brought with them a fresher current of air and had nothing provincial about them.

It was in Göttingen that we experienced the effects of Hitler's seizure of power. They no longer came as a surprise. At that time we read, 'Tens of thousands from all political camps, from all professions and classes, lined the streets and felt themselves at one in spirit with the brown soldiers of the Third Reich who were greeted with tempestuous cries of "Heil!". Anyone who saw the members of the S.A. and S.S., some three thousand strong, and the Hitler Youth marching by, caught up in the impetus of an inspiring movement and yet united in iron discipline, and in addition the many who marched with them in the rhythm of the Prussian marches must have felt that this was a great moment in history.'

At first the semester continued undisturbed. But immediately after the Reichstag fire of 1933, which the Nazis in fact explained as a communist attack, the first steps were already taken in the removal of essential basic rights: the freedom of the individual, the right to keep one's correspondence confidential, the inviolability of the home, the freedom of the Press, freedom to join associations, freedom to assemble, as well as the security of private property.

Very soon the hope, so eagerly nourished, that Hitler would soon ruin himself by mis-management was shattered. National Socialism established itself with lightning swiftness. It was supported financially by industry and given an intellectual underpinning and made presentable by the universities where so many jurists came forward with new theories of jurisprudence. There were also some who believed that they could act as mediators, but most of these soon joined the Nazis. On the 7th April, National Socialist administrators were set up over member states of the German Reich and the law for the so-called 'restoration of the professional civil service' was imposed, debarring 'non-Aryans' from the service of the state. By the end of April a secret state police was in being. The 'Enabling Act' cleared the way for Hitler to impose his rule without restraint.

In Göttingen, too, the so-called 'restoration of the professional civil service' now began to make itself felt. The faculty of the natural sciences was outstandingly rich in talent with figures such as James Franck, Born, Landau, Weyl, Hilbert, Courant and others. The effects of this law upon this faculty were particularly strong. At that time the pressure of circumstances which we all felt in common brought us, too, into closer contact with the natural scientists who were being persecuted for reasons of race. We discussed the terror, the future, and the possibilities of emigrating to other countries.

Another sign of the times was the increase in foreign correspondence with colleagues engaged in the same fields of study abroad. Many close acquaintants, former fellow students, and friends and teachers of Gert's were in fact by now scattered to the four winds. In those days it was already a matter of doubt whether these letters which one received from abroad had not passed through the hands of the Gestapo, and this gave us a great feeling of insecurity.

After the close of the semester we travelled to Berlin, stayed with our parents, and made it our first task to visit my father-in-law, who at that time was sixty-five and seriously ill. Even on his deathbed he still had to experience his dismissal as an alderman by the Nazis and see his eldest son, Hans, thrown out of his post as a judge.

This April of 1933, which we were still intending to spend in Berlin, saw fresh and monstrous measures brought into force. On the 1st April a boycott was organized against Jewish stores. My grandmother Bonhoeffer, who was in her ninetieth year, saw the S.A. men standing in front of a store with placards saying 'Germans defend yourselves! Do not buy from Jews!' The store had not closed. When the S.A. men tried to restrain her from entering she simply said, 'I buy the things I need where I like', and slipped into the store. Again in the city when she came to the Kaufhaus des Westens she ignored the picket line of the S.A. demonstrating before it and entered the store unhesitatingly to make her purchases.

In 1936 our grandmother Bonhoeffer died, and Dietrich preached the funeral sermon over her. Among other things he said of her:

'A refusal to compromise over the right principle, free speech for the free individual, the fact that one's word once given is binding, clarity and common sense in one's opinions, candour and simplicity of life in private and in public—these were factors that went to her very heart. ... She could not bear to see these values despised or to see the rights of an individual violated. For this reason her last years were clouded with the great sorrow that she bore for the fate of the Jews among our people, a burden which she shared with them and a suffering which she, too, felt. She stemmed from another age, from another spiritual world, and this world does not descend with her into the grave. ... This heritage for which we thank her lays duties upon us.'

Of course we also visited Gert's relatives, all of whom had their deep anxieties. A cousin of my husband's was a high judge in Berlin and had been decorated with the Iron Cross First Class in the First World War. He, too, was thrown out of his office. Later he was taken by the S.S. and together with his wife put in the camp at Theresienstadt where he died shortly afterwards. His wife, who became ill there, was transferred to the liquidation centre at Auschwitz to be put in the gas chamber. Gert's other cousin took his own life. His wife and fourteen-year-old daughter escaped to Belgium, but then after the Germans had occupied it, they, too, were carried off to Auschwitz and murdered there. Gert's best friend at school drowned himself in the Gardasee.

The moment we arrived home at Göttingen after the funeral of my father-in-law, and before we had so much as taken off our overcoats, we received a telephone call from the dean of the faculty of law at Göttingen to the effect that my husband should not take part in the May-day procession. Otherwise disturbances would ensue. My husband replied that he had not intended to join the procession and that he would be happy not to take part in the march, and that the dedication of the Nazi banner at the university was of no interest to him. The dean was one of those countless thousands who were driven into the arms of National Socialism by ambition. In spite of his age he was still striving to obtain a professorship at Berlin and later actually received one.

Every day it became more unpleasant. At the instigation of the National Socialist student leaders and students my husband's lectures, which had been extremely well attended, were to be boycotted. Even the dean informed my husband that a boycott would take place. I was anxious lest Gert should be forced to endure some kind of mobbing and tried to dissuade him from holding this course of lectures. Gert was intending to talk on 'The Image of the State in the Twentieth Century' and it had already been announced. The party regarded this subject as 'provocation'.

At that time I had often heard my husband's lectures and I went to the university on the actual day of the boycott in order to be there and to hear what the students would have to say. A few students were standing there in S.A. uniform, straddling the doorway with their jackboots as only these S.A. men could and not allowing anyone to enter. 'Leibholz must not lecture, he is a Jew. The lectures are not taking place.' Obediently the students went home. A corresponding notice had been posted on the blackboard. The matter was also reported in the Press. The curator had to give his support to the immediate removal of pictures of eminent Jewish scholars.

Obviously it had long become impossible to appeal to any sense of justice. The S.P.D. (Social Democrats) had been forbidden. The transition from the trade unions to the 'labour front' had been accomplished. The 'national community' was one of the most powerful of all slogans. The other parties dissolved themselves of their own accord. The universities did not hold out as the Dutch universities did. In 1940, the university of Leyden closed because a 'non-Aryan' member of the teaching staff lost his post. In Göttingen many tried to collaborate. Lecturers who had not achieved further promotion now saw their opportunity. Many senior members were anxious not to be thrust aside as 'ossified' and often behaved in a most unworthy manner. Thank God, there were also some men of integrity among the professors. Once again we found ourselves thrown together with the victims of political persecution and becoming part of their group. A figure whom I particularly remember was the theologian, Walter Bauer. When we met him in the street he did not cross to the other side—as people very often did—but came up to my husband and abused Hitler and the Nazis. Since he had bad hearing his utterances on this subject were often so loud and clear that in my anxiety I used to cast 'German' glances right and left, fearful lest anyone should hear him. The elderly Örtmann, professor of civil law, came to us at once as soon as my husband was deprived of his post. 'Sir, you are my colleague and I am ashamed to be a German,' said he with tears in his eyes and shaking us both by the hand. Again, a group of students who were participating in my husband's seminar tried to intervene with the Ministry and asked for Gert to be allowed to remain in his post.

Since my husband had not yet been officially dismissed he began, despite all difficulties, to give his course of lectures once more, and it was remarkable that he was actually able to continue lecturing unmolested for a considerable time. Admittedly uniformed Nazis were sitting here and there on the benches, which was not very comfortable for me. Finally Gert sent in his resignation in order to anticipate his dismissal. Subsequently all 'non-Aryans' were prohibited from entering the university or the university library. 'It is not the over-cultivated intellects, not the master-minds in the professorial chairs that have chased out the "relative" Einsteins, the Hirschfelds and their lot, but our fists.' This statement appeared in the University Journal of Lower Saxony.

In almost every village in Lower Saxony a notice was now to be seen conspicuously displayed and saying 'Jews not Desired',

'There is Nothing Here for Jews', 'Jews Get Out'. Once when our little Marianne saw such a placard being set up just next to the village crucifix she cried out 'Just look! Right next to the Lord Jesus!'

On Remembrance Sunday Dietrich wrote to us. When my father-in-law died Dietrich had been persuaded by the authorities under whom he worked not to conduct the funeral service because my father-in-law was of the Jewish faith. And he was now remorseful for having accepted this advice. My husband had wanted it because my father-in-law, whose children had been baptized Protestants, did not attend the synagogue himself and he had esteemed Dietrich very highly.

Dear Gert, dear Sabine,

I would so much like to write to you for next Sunday. I was just working at my sermon for Remembrance Sunday, and am forcibly reminded again and again of you and of those days in March. What a wonderful text that is that occurs in the Wisdom of Solomon chapter 3:1 ff. Just read it for yourselves! I am going to preach simply on the few words which run 'But they are in peace'. That would have been the right text for your father! Now it is a matter of constant remorse to me that at that time I did not quite simply accede to your request. Frankly I no longer understand myself in the least. How could I have been so horribly timid at that time? Certainly you have not really understood this either, and have not said anything to me about it. But it haunts me now as something quite dreadful, the more so because it is precisely something which now can never be made good. Today, therefore I must simply beg you to forgive me for this weakness of mine at the time. Today I know for sure that I should have acted otherwise. This time one feels the message of Remembrance Sunday particularly poignantly because after all that has taken place in these last months one feels so deep a longing for that real and ultimate peace in which the sorrow, the injustice, the lies and the cowardice are at last truly brought to an end, where the struggle ceases and all is quiet, held by a strong hand. Yet it is certainly dangerous to allow oneself to be carried away by such promptings and one still has to live by hope as before. We really must not be despondent. Dear Gert, I believe that your father would probably have lived through even such a time as this with a much greater zest for the future, a more resolute refusal to be discouraged, than is the case with most of us. And yet as your brother Hans said at the time, it must be so beautiful to have peace. In fact you do have an element of such peace in your house with your children, and I have an element of it in the community to which I minister, and indeed we really must be thankful for this. May all go very well with you. I think so often of you even though I only write infrequently. Thank you so much for your letters. In spite of the calendar, dear Gert, I have forgotten your birthday in the upheaval of moving. Forgive me!

My special love to the children and warmest love to yourselves,

Yours, Dietrich

In 1934 we brought a car so as to have some means of transport in case of urgent need. We absented ourselves from Göttingen as often as possible, frequently staying in Berlin with my parents or going abroad, and even at this stage always with emigration in mind.

As far as possible, too, we removed the children from school in order to spare them unpleasant incidents. Three times our little Marianne at seven years old was sent back by the school porter because she said 'Good morning' and not 'Heil Hitler', also for failing to raise her arm. Finally when he set up a great bellowing at her she did so. On the whole she was able to stick up for herself. She was a sensible child, good at her school work, and she always had one or two little girls with whom she could still be friends. About 1934 she received the following postcard from Dietrich:

Dear little Marianne,

All my good wishes for your birthday! I wish you a happy new year, that you may make your parents very happy, that you may be a good elder sister to Christiane, that you may go on telling and writing down such beautiful stories, and then I hope we can have nice conversations together just as we did recently at your home. Your mother will let you have something from me and I hope it will give you pleasure. What a very fine thing it is when one becomes big enough gradually to begin doing something which can help other people. And you can do this already! With warmest love,

Your uncle, Dietrich

Then the time came when our little Christiane also had to go to school. Their schoolfellows began to whisper about our children. One little friend actually called out to her over the fence, 'Your father is a Jew'. A teacher said to one of the pupils in front of the whole class, 'Do not talk so much with your hands. Only Marianne Leibholz may do that!', And this in the child's presence! One day a notice-board was fixed to one of the trees in front of the school on which was written 'The Father of the Jew is the Devil'. Every day our two children passed under this piece of rabble-rousing on their way to school. Then a box with the Nazi newspaper *Der Stürmer* with its abominations was set up opposite the school. It contained anti-Semitic matter, fantastic accounts of sexual crimes and sadistic ritual acts allegedly practised by the Jews and fabricated stories of the most obscene kind. The elder school children thronged in front of this.

We were glad that we did not have to let our daughters become members of the Hitler Youth. But on the other hand this in itself naturally had an isolating effect upon them among their classmates. Dietrich's letters constantly restored our spirits. His optimism, which he cultivated even though his future, too, was so uncertain, did us good. He wrote to us from London:

Dear Gert,

I am really sorry that recently I gave you such a fright during the night and in fact it was exceptionally stupid. In spite of this, however, it was very pleasant to speak with you once more and to hear that things are going well with you. First, therefore, every good wish for next year! One does not know which one wishes more, much peace on the one hand or much change on the other. I am so very sorry that you are having anxieties about the children. Sabine wrote about this. I send her my warmest thanks for her dear letter and the little parcel. But in such a case why do you not send the children straightaway to Berlin in the car to stay with one of our brothers or sisters or with our parents? I really don't understand this. Next week I will come to Berlin, and then probably for a longer visit in January on leave from here, even though not yet for good. What will happen after that I do not yet know. I have made myself very much at home here and yet naturally my life's work does not lie here. I do not like leaving, but more from certain feelings of security which are very *bourgeois* and these must certainly not be allowed to become a major factor, otherwise life will no longer have any real value at all and there will no longer be any joy in it either. So I hope to see you again soon. Forgive me for being so brief. I must make haste to leave and this letter must be on time.

Every good wish to all of you together,

Yours, Dietrich

Like the houses of many of the professors, our house was situated in the Herzberger Landstrasse. On Sunday mornings the S.A. liked to march through this fine, broad residential street. Even today it still makes me shudder to remember their marching songs, 'Soldiers, comrades, hang the Jews, shoot the Jews'. At first the Horst-Wessel song was also still sung, the 'Germany awake!' and also 'Today Germany belongs to us, tomorrow the whole world'. After the shameless Nüremberg Laws, which revealed all too plainly the obscene imagination of the Nazis, we were no longer allowed to keep our housemaids, kitchen maids or the nursemaid, all of whom were very close to one another. There were tears. From now onwards the housemaids had to be more than forty-five years old. Even before this the housemaids were already being harried whenever they were found to be working in Jewish or half-Jewish households. S.A. messengers in uniform who delivered the goods would say, for instance, 'What, are you still working with Jews?' And to the rejoinder, 'Here they are all Christians', the lout would reply, 'Aha, Jews in disguise!' The same thing would then be repeated in the form of pressure from the girl's young man or friends, who began to be anxious about their jobs if they were in the labour service or wanted to find advancement elsewhere. The number of the professors from whom we still received visits had grown smaller. A colleague who had become our friend was a great disappointment to us, for one fine day he joined the S.S. simply from motives of opportunism—he used to laugh at the S.S.—and quite openly announced to us, 'So from now on I can only come to you after dark'. More than fifty professors of the University of Göttingen had now been expelled from the teaching body.

On the 14th August 1935 we received a letter from Ernst Neustadt, formerly headmaster of the Goethe School at Frankfurt and Marianne's god-father. In this, amongst other things, he described with utter horror the slogans painted on the cars used in processions in Munich and the songs that went with these: 'German man and German woman, do not buy from Jewish swine!' and further, 'Jesuit means parasite' and 'Rather be a heathen than a Catholic currency profiteer'. Neustadt emigrated to England. Later he hanged himself there.

The first time I heard through my sister Christel von Dohnanyi (whose husband had told her about it) what was going on in the concentration camps, I was so anxious that I was unwilling to hear any more. But thenceforward I did want to know what attitude was adopted towards the National Socialist régime by those with whom I had personal contacts. I had the feeling that one had to reach far and wide to find men of integrity. There seemed to be hardly any left in this world in which we were still trying to go on living with our family. We now began to look about for those who shared our political outlook and felt a great longing to find others of the same mind as ourselves. And, thank God, even in Germany we still did find individuals who thought as we did and as our families did. But where were those who were willing to take action? Fichte's fine saying was forgotten: 'And you must act as though the fate of German affairs depended upon you and your action alone, and as though the responsibility were yours.'

I have an unpleasant memory of a visit by the Department for Investigating Currency Offences to inspect our safe. One day we received news that we had to open this in the presence of two officials from this Department. I went down to the safe with the two men and opened it, and they made the most detailed examination of everything. But having found nothing there to which they could take exception they departed again. There were two men of integrity at the 'Commerz' bank who let us have exactly the same amount of foreign currency as all other customers, and that in itself was a great favour. One of these was Willi

Drescher, a devout Baptist and on Christian principles an outspoken enemy of the Nazis. The other was a Jewish man named Hammerschlag who, probably because of his great ability, could not be replaced all that quickly. It was these who opened the gates of freedom to us. In the midst of his activities as director of the Pastors' Seminary, Dietrich wrote to me for my birthday:

Dear Sabine,

What a pity that yet again we cannot celebrate our birthday together! I had so looked forward to it. I believe that we have not managed it since we were twenty. Unfortunately on this particular day I shall myself be rather harassed. I shall only be in Berlin for a few hours, the rest of the time on the road and in the Seminary where, as I fear, many preparations are already in progress. I don't really like to be the centre of a celebration when I have contributed nothing whatever to making it possible. On the other hand, however, it is pleasant to see that other people like to avail themselves of an occasion for celebrating. Life for the young theologians is today of such a kind that one is glad about every occasion they have to enjoy themselves. Who knows how often they may still have such pleasures? We think that after the Olympics many matters will be clarified. We don't mind this, but of course this is easily said beforehand. Don't you think the last ten years have really been very deeply rewarding for us? You know that in spite of everything I would rather be alive today than thirty years ago. I wonder whether really this is not also the case with you, Sabine, and with you both—provided, that is, one can manage to look a little beyond the personal dimension and thereby discern all kinds of promising factors which have been brought into being precisely today and were not in being thirty years ago. One asks whether here and there in the 'flux of time', and specifically among our children too, that 'character formation' is not being achieved for which we hope for later times. In these days I am again thinking a great deal about Grandmama's death. It was like the end of an epoch! From her way of living we can, after all, learn so much for today. Now I wish you and all of you a very happy day. Let each of us wish the other that as brother and sister we may continue to remain as close to one another as we have been up to the present. Certainly we shall still have great need of one another.

My warmest love to you, together with Gert and the children,

Yours, Dietrich

There were times when my nerves were jangled at every ring on the bell, for towards evening individual Jews were 'visited' here and there and we even heard stories of some of them being driven through the streets in their nightshirts while others were rounded up and taken away. One evening at about eleven o'clock our doorbell rang and I was terribly frightened. I called out to my husband to get away through the large garden at the back in case something unpleasant was going to happen. But it was only two S.A. men who had come with their 'Heil Hitler' and raised arms to ask for some kind of information.

As a result of the allowances of foreign currency granted to us we were able to make several more journeys with the children to Switzerland. Once beyond the German borders we even managed to sleep better again. We lived for one winter month in Grindelwald amidst the magic of a landscape with mountains and snow. Softly gliding rides in the sleigh with the snorting horses before us, great flakes of snow falling slow and quiet, a profound stillness, black pinewoods, the lights shining from distant windows—at a time when there was still hardly any tourist trade, one could still enjoy all this—together with the dazzling sunshine, the warmth of the sun on our backs by the middle of the day, our children with their attempts at skiing, never a brownshirt in sight but all the more Englishmen for that, pursuing every branch of sport without conceit and enjoying themselves in the sun like children! We were also at Locarno with the children for a longer period and spent several weeks more in Lenzerheide. In Holland, too, we put out our feelers. The Dutch did a great deal for the refugees. Gert's brother was now living at the Hague with his wife. Glad as he was to be able to live in freedom again, he suffered under the changed circumstances in which he was forced to exist. Each time that we journeyed back to Göttingen something like an iron band seemed to tighten round my heart with every kilometre that brought us nearer to the town.

At about this time my father wrote as follows:

'The victory of National Socialism in 1933 and the appoint-ment of Hitler as Chancellor of the Reich were events which we regarded from the outset as a disaster, and in fact all members of the family were unanimous in this. In my case I disliked and mistrusted Hitler because of his demagogic propa-ganda speeches, his telegram of sympathy on the occasion of the Potempa murder, his journeys by car through the country, horsewhip in hand, his choice of colleagues, about whose qualities we here in Berlin may have had a more detailed knowledge than those elsewere, and finally because of what I heard from my professional colleagues regarding his psychopathic symptoms.

'In 1918 after the general breakdown, conditions at the Charité Clinic had also at first been difficult, but in a rela-tively short time, and after lively discussions with regard to the eight-hour day, it soon became possible once more to work quietly without any material hindrance from the political authorities. This time it was different. Young medical trainees, hitherto unknown, came as authorized representatives of the Party and approached the directors of the hospital with a demand that they should immediately dismiss the Jewish doctors. Some among them allowed themselves to be influenced by this. Any attempt to point out that it was not the Party but the Ministry which had to take decisions in such matters was answered with threats. In the faculty the dean attempted to induce the members to join the Party as a collective group. Thanks to the resistance of some individuals it was possible to avert this. Again with regard to the dismissal of Jewish assistants which had been demanded, the Ministry at first held back. But the individual hospitals continued to be subjected to systematic spying with regard to the attitude of the doctors towards the Party. Professional relationships between the doctors belonging to the hospital, hitherto undisturbed, were to a large extent destroyed by mutual mistrust. Probably the Party had a confidential agent in every hospital who would report to the Party about the individual doctors and about the assistants to be appointed without informing the director of the hospital of what he was doing. On the whole it can be said of my hospital that the majority of the assistants withstood the pres-sure. But the hospital was a thorn in the flesh to the "leadership of the university teachers". Right up to my departure in 1938, I managed to prevent a picture of Hitler being set up in the Charité. Probably it was the only hospital in which this was the case. But to make up for this, when my successor arrived he set up a larger bust than usual in the vestibule of the clinic.

'So far as scientific activities are concerned, I see from my records covering the period 1896-1940 that 1933 was the only year in which no scientific publication by me appeared. Clearly there was on the one hand a lack of that interior tranquillity which is an essential condition for maintaining an uninterrupted flow of scientific work, while on the other the law for "The Prevention of Hereditary Diseases in Future Generations" issued in July 1933 made it urgent to test the effects of this law from the point of view of psychiatry. The question of the sterilization of the mentally subnormal had been the subject of lively public discussion in individual states in America since the beginning of the century, and since 1909 had actually been expressed in legal form there. Thus it is not, as has often been believed in recent times, an invention of National Socialism. When, in 1932, the discussion of the question was renewed it gave rise to a proposal from the Regional Board of Health in Prussia to institute a law of freedom from hereditary disease. This was conveyed to the Ministry of Welfare but in it the agreement of the patient remained a necessary condition for surgical intervention in every case. The law of the 15th June 1933 went beyond all the proposals that had previously been made and all the legal decisions that had been arrived at elsewhere by introducing the element of compulsion. The danger of mistaken judgements by inadequately trained doctors was great—the more so since in the beginning it was not infrequently the case that the only specialist qualification taken into consideration in choosing the specialists for this was membership of the Party. In my own immediate circle I had experience of this when one day one of the young medical trainees attached to my hospital, who was still inexperienced in psychiatry, informed me that at the instigation of the doctors' leader, Conti, he had been appointed as the medical specialist member of the tribunal for freedom from hereditary disease. He had insight enough immediately to resign from this position at my instigation. It can surely be regarded as certain that in many places there were no adequately trained psychiatrists. Any withdrawal of the compulsion clause was inconceivable, given the National Socialist mentality. And thus the only possibility remaining open was to restrict its application, and, through publications and instructional procedures in psychiatry, to draw attention to the special difficulties of diagnosis involved in dealing with this area of "freedom from hereditary disease".

'Up till then, in view of my academic functions, I had as far as possible withdrawn myself from the practice of psychiatry at the forensic level. But now it seemed to me to be demanded of me that I should take over the position of the specialist psychiatrist in the Chief Court for Freedom from Hereditary Disease in order that I might have some influence upon the judgements of the courts. In fact—and I have received confirmation of this from many sides—the result of this was that in Berlin and also in the provinces considerable prudence was exercised in the processes by which diagnostic judgements were arrived at. The lectures and publications of the Berlin hospital in the field of the psychiatric aspects of heredity were unfavourably received in the "Braune Haus" at Munich. After two years the Ministry of the Interior no longer permitted the lectures to continue.

'One of the points envisaged in the law was that the doctor was bound to notify the existence of any hereditary disease. With regard to this I was unable to consent to any setting aside of the doctor's duty to preserve professional secrecy, and in fact never notified the existence of any illness discovered in my consulting room to the medical authorities. After 1933, the only official ceremony in the university in which I took any further part was the first address of Herr Rust, the Minister for Culture at the university. Unfortunately on this occasion neither I nor the other professors had the courage to leave the lecture-room as a protest against the insulting attitude of the Minister towards the professors. At all later public ceremonies and official addresses I absented myself.

'I was commissioned to examine and give an opinion upon Lubbe, the perpetrator of the Reichstag fire. In the course of this task I had an opportunity to make the acquaintance of a whole series of prominent Party members. They had come together in great numbers on the occasion of the trial before the Supreme Court at Leipzig. The types of faces one saw on this occasion were for the most part very unpleasant. During the hearings the calm and the painstaking objectivity of the President of the court were in striking and agreeable contrast to the insolence of the Party members who were interrogated. Dimitrov, who was one of the accused, gave an impression of intellectual superiority. He sent Goering, the Minister President who had been invited, into a state of uncontrollable fury. Lubbe was a case of a young man who, though psychopathic, was humanly speaking not altogether unlikeable, a muddle-headed adventurer who, in the course of the proceedings, fell into a defiant stupor from which he only emerged shortly before his execution.'

We ought to have left Germany long ago, but we can judge our decisions only in the perspective of the actual time at which they were taken. Amazingly we again and again found reasons for postponing our emigration in spite of terrifying news which our brother-in-law, Hans von Dohnanyi, caused to be brought to us with a view to inducing us to undertake the emigration before it was too late. The fresh threat with which we were now suddenly confronted was the possibility of my husband losing his passport. At the end of August 1938 we felt that a serious European crisis was at hand, that perhaps very soon it might come to war. Accordingly we prepared ourselves to leave Germany. The great upheaval involved in making concrete plans was initiated. But Gert's spirit was so weighed down that often he was quite incapable of thinking out the most important questions calmly. He walked many kilometres round our large garden; sometimes I could hardly bear to watch him, so troubled with all our decisions. Again and again when we seemed to be quite near to the decision, fresh considerations would arise among them being the fact that in their desire to preserve peace the Western Powers failed to stand up to Hitler. One asked oneself, 'Does it still make sense to emigrate to a country within Europe?'

When fears increased that Hitler would put into practice 'his ultimate territorial demand', the occupation of Czechoslovakia, we left Germany. We travelled on the 9th September 1938. Even

then our departure was still a precipitate one. We arrived at
the border at Basle about ten o'clock in the evening. The customs
officials were too tired to do much questioning or to search us
thoroughly. Beforehand I had had great anxiety in thinking of
what would happen at the border. I had dreaded the thorough
searches imposed by the Nazi customs officials of which we had
heard, but we were very lucky. Dietrich and Eberhard Bethge had
accompanied us as far as Giessen.

My daughter Marianne describes our exodus from her own
memories:

'In the summer of 1938 I gathered from tiny hints thrown
out by my mother that my parents were definitely preparing
to leave Germany. I was just eleven. I knew about the Czech
crisis and that there might be a war, that the likelihood of
war was growing every day, that we did not want to be
caught in Germany in a war because then we would no longer
be able to leave the country if necessary. I knew that any
plans to leave should be kept absolutely secret, and that if my
parents told me no more than they did they had their reasons.
I watched for hints of anything unusual in our lives, and on
days when I got a strong feeling that something ominous
would soon be happening I put several large or small crosses
in my diary according to the strength of my suspicions.

'On August 23rd my parents went to my grandparents in
Berlin for four days and Great-Aunt Elizabeth von Hase came
to supervise the household. On August 31st my father went
to Hamburg for the day, on September 4th my parents left
for Berlin, returning late on September 8th with Uncle Dietrich
Bonhoeffer and Pastor Eberhard Bethge. On all these days I
put down huge crosses.

'The morning of September 9th was gloriously sunny in
Göttingen. As usual, our Nanny woke up my seven-year-old
sister Christiane and me at half-past six and began to help
us to dress for school. Suddenly my mother came into the
night nursery in a great hurry and said, "You're not going
to school today, we're going to Wiesbaden", and to our Nanny,
"We'll be back on Monday. The children are to wear two lots
of underclothes each".

'I knew at once that something very serious was happening

97

to us. My parents never went to Wiesbaden, this was obviously said to mislead our Nanny, and never before had we had to wear two lots of underclothes. I said to myself: "We're leaving; as we can't take more out of the country than goes into the car and we have hardly any money abroad, wearing two lots of underclothes is an inconspicuous way of getting some extra clothes out of the country." I tore downstairs and ran round the whole of our huge garden saying good-bye to it. I wanted to say goodbye to all the rooms in the house, but feared the adults would guess I knew what was up and confined my good-byes to one floor. I collected two finger-length dolls, their passports and certificates of birth and baptism which I had previously made, crayons, my diary; these would go into my pocket. I realized that any big toys would take up valuable car space. My best friend, Sybille von Schönfeldt, came rushing up the stairs; we always walked to school together. "You aren't ready! We'll be late for school!" "I'm not coming, we're going to Wiesbaden for three days." She stared at me, astonished and disappointed. "Oh, well, good-bye then, I must dash." I looked after her hard, thinking I must remember forever what she looked like.

'Our car was very full, but packed to look as if we were going on a normal holiday. Christiane and I were embedded in the back. Uncle Dietrich and "Uncle" Bethge had brought another car, Uncle Dietrich's, and during the drive my parents and the uncles sat in the front seats of the two cars, changing places frequently, so that all came to sit with us children in turns.

'We stopped briefly in Göttingen where the men bought a giant torch for the journey. When we were out of the town my mother said, "We're not going to Wiesbaden, we're trying to get across the Swiss border tonight. They may close the frontier because of the crisis".

The roof of our car was open, the sky was deep blue, the countryside looked marvellous in the hot sunshine. I felt there was complete solidarity between the four grown-ups. I knew that unaccustomed things would be asked of us children from now on but felt proud of now being allowed to share the real troubles of the adults. I thought that if I could do nothing against the Nazis myself I must at the very least co-operate with the grown-ups who could. Christiane and I spent most of the time singing in the car, folk songs and rather militant songs about freedom, my mother, Uncle Dietrich and "Uncle" Bethge singing with us. I enjoyed the various descants. Uncle Dietrich taught me a new round, *Über die Wellen gleitet der Kahn.*

'During the drive, my uncle seemed to me just as I always remember him: very strong and confident, immensely kind, cheerful and firm.

'We stopped at Giessen and picnicked by the wayside. The grown-ups' mood did not strike me as depressing. Then all of a sudden they said it was getting late and that we must hurry. "We have to get across the frontier tonight, they may close it at any moment." We children settled in our car, our parents got in, and I remember Uncle Dietrich and "Uncle" Bethge waving farewell to us until they became tiny and were cut off by a hill. The rest of the drive was no longer cheerful. My parents drove as fast as they could, we stopped talking so that they could concentrate. The atmosphere was tense.

'We crossed the Swiss border late at night. Christiane and I pretended to be asleep and very angry at being wakened, to discourage the German frontier guards from doing too much searching of the car. My mother had put on a long, very brown suede jacket, whose brownness was meant to pacify the German officials. They let our car through and the Swiss let us in. My parents were not to cross the German border again till after the war.

'The sense of liberation after leaving German soil and entering a free country was so overwhelming in those days that an echo of that feeling still returns now, so many years later, whenever I cross the German frontier into Switzerland.'

We now drove on in the car to Zürich, in order to hear all the news promptly during the crisis, and took up our quarters in a hotel on the Zürichberg. Three times a day we drove down in order to read the newspapers. They were magical autumn days but one's enjoyment of them was only remote, as a sick man experiences what the weather is like from his bed.

We knew from our brother-in-law, Hans von Dohnanyi, that a plan was being introduced for 'non-Aryans' to have their passports marked 'J'. And since we were anxious not to find ourselves shut in in Germany by an untimely return with all the possibly terrible consequences for my husband, we had asked our parents to send us a telegram with the codeword *passt* as soon as the 'J' plan was put into operation. And now the telegram arrived: 'Your coming is not convenient (*passt*) at present'. Then we knew that we could no longer return to Germany. We sent a telegram to our parents that we would like to travel further, and after a few days my kind sister Ursula appeared in Zürich laden with packages and with my fur coat over her arm in order to take back the children to my parents in Berlin for the time being (for they were not affected by the difficulty over the passports) until we had found a foothold in England. We also sent our car, an almost new Ford, back to Germany in order not to incur immediate annoyances at the hands of the National Socialist authorities at Göttingen. For at that time only very few professors had cars and the absence of our car would quickly be remarked upon.

We journeyed through France to England. The journey to Calais seemed to me endless and colourless. We longed to get to England, which received us in fog. A pastor who was a friend of ours had sent us an invitation and we travelled to London together with the luggage which we had managed to bring with us in the car on our exodus. We had never been in England up to that point. In earlier times we had always travelled in a more southerly direction so that we were now arriving in a land which was completely unfamiliar to us.

PART THREE

OUR LIFE IN ENGLAND AS REFUGEES FROM HITLER

13

First contacts in London

The soil of our homeland draws us all with its sweetness
And never lets us forget what it means to us.
The beginning of virtue consists in learning
The fact that the tried and tested spirit
Learns first to recognize
That these visible homelands
Are transitory,
To exchange them for a time for other lands,
And finally to leave them for ever.
He to whom his fatherland is sweet
Is still tender.
But he to whom the soil of every land is mother earth
Is strong.
He only is perfect to whom the whole world is a place of exile
From my childhood upwards
I have been an exile,
And I know what affliction it causes,
What spirit it requires,
To leave that narrow environment
Which is one's very own,
And later what freedom it is
To view the marble palaces
With detachment.
                    Hugh of St Victor, Twelfth century.

The journey to London passed very quietly. The passengers

did not speak to one another. The men were absorbed in their evening papers and puffing away at their pipes. Every now and then there would be a murmur of 'sorry' as one of them brushed slightly against his neighbour in the act of turning the pages. A feeling arose in me that from now onwards I could no longer foresee anything. When we arrived at Victoria Station we were overwhelmed. The babble of alien voices, the jostling of the crowds, the speed with which the hurrying porters attended to the new arrivals and their questions, which were incomprehensible to us, the taxis which came driving right up to the platform, the smells—it was all very strange.

We were met by Pastor Boeckheler, a man whom I had known from the days of my youth at Tübingen. Once we had had rowing expeditions on the Neckar together, and I had spent happy musical evenings at his family home. Now he was Pastor of the German congregation at Sydenham, having succeeded my brother Dietrich in that post. He lived in the same Victorian pastor's house at Forest Hill which my brother had left on the resumption of his work in the Confessing Church in Germany.

Our journey through the city took three quarters of an hour. It was already dark. The lights shone dully through the London fog of that November evening and the atmosphere was in tune with my mood. Straightaway we received our first and overwhelming impression of the 'rush hour', with its great torrents of humanity.

The boarding house where we were to live was conducted by a Miss Sharp, a hard-working and likeable Methodist lady, and was situated in south-east London, surrounded by an old garden which was full of trees. It was an old house, scrupulously clean but impractical, which could accommodate about fifteen boarders. Here in the mornings, dressed in a bright blue overall, and with a cap of the same colour on her silver-grey hair, Miss Sharp was to be seen armed with her feather duster, often humming gentle tunes to herself as she worked. At midday, Miss Sharp transformed herself into an attentive hostess and in the afternoon she presided over the tea, a meal which took place in the drawing-room. She also gave piano lessons in the afternoons and saw to the preparation of dinner. Later still, she would attend the church choir of her Methodist community. This was a new world into which we had been transferred. None of the other boarders spoke a single word of German. My husband could speak only very little English. In his school, which had concentrated upon the humanities, English had been taught by the gym instructor! As Werner Finck, the cabaret artist, has said, 'English enough to get you through school—yes. But heaven help you once you went abroad!' My English was a little better.

We occupied a room with twin beds which had three fine large sash windows, though it must be said that the wind blew strongly through these, and the rattling of them would not have allowed us to sleep had we not stuck some pieces of wood between the sashes. Our bedrooms were without heat the entire winter through. There was, it is true, a gas fire, which we used to keep alight during the day by putting a shilling into a meter every now and then. But one had to sit close to it in order to feel any warmth. The room itself was always cold. The utmost heat which we could achieve was twelve degrees centigrade. We soon fell into a general attitude of 'putting up with things as they were'. One learnt that in winter one would be frozen and one found one's own solutions to the problem of cold. One also accustomed oneself to damp, which made one enervated but was the secret of the beauty alike of English meadows and English skins. In one respect the life was probably unhealthy. One drank one's ten to twelve cups of hot tea—and one drank them strong! It gave one warmth and 'go'. The foggy days with darkness closing in early and the street lamps outside with their own peculiar atmosphere somehow had a calming effect upon us and brought some degree of composure to our troubled spirits. For anxieties as to what the future might hold and whether we would find any kind of suitable work for Gert preyed upon us ceaselessly.

On the first morning we looked round the district in which we had found our initial foothold. Then in the afternoon we embarked straightaway upon the task of making contacts. Dietrich had given us all the addresses of his acquaintances and friends, and that same afternoon we already found ourselves sitting on the upper deck of a red bus, being transported through London's populace, past dwelling houses, offices and parks into the city, a journey of forty-five minutes. One usually began by foregathering in the 'Strand', a hotel which was particularly favoured by refugees and foreigners, and the conversation constantly turned upon the same anxieties. A number of refugees who had arrived earlier, in 1933, had already found some sort of occupation. While in very many cases the work they were doing was below the level of their abilities or education, they had found a niche and their future had begun. However this did not apply to the lawyers. We heard of a judge who was sweeping the streets and an advocate who was a lift attendant. We proceeded to make numerous visits. We sought out Dietrich's English acquaintances, above all English lawyers, but could nowhere discover any work suitable for a professor of constitutional law. At the time we were only just beginning, and still cherished our illusions.

We had hardly been in England a few days when we heard the extremely disquieting news of the pogrom which had taken place in Germany on the 9th November 1938. Our children were still in Berlin with my parents. In Göttingen, the following account appeared: 'We in Göttingen have no need to be silent concerning what took place on the night of the 10th November 1938. Those who do not show understanding of it are incapable of comprehending the voice of the people. We have seen the temple of the vindictive god of the Jews in Upper Maschstrasse going up in flames.... In view of very recent events there must be nothing in our city either to remind us of this race, which is worse than a plague raging through the peoples of the earth.'

According to word-of-mouth reports it was the S.A. students who played the chief part in these pogroms, in the course of which Jews were subjected to harassment of the most disgraceful kind. For instance a storm troop of S.A. students smashed the valuable collection of porcelain belonging to a Jewish acquaintance of ours. On the morning following the 'Crystal Night', a university lecturer was greeted by a porter with the words: 'What a pity that you were not there last night to join in, Herr Doctor. You missed something there!'

The reaction in England to the burning of the synagogues was one of great horror. Soon we heard more detailed accounts of the 'Crystal Night', how Jews had been arrested and Jewish businesses had been destroyed. The day following this, Dietrich wrote to us. Since our children were still in Berlin he made no mention of these events.

10.11.1938

Dear Sabine, dear Gert,

Many thanks for the greetings you send me from my erst-while community. I am glad that you have been so kindly received and have already had your first invitations. Once one has become a little more accustomed to life there one feels more favourably disposed towards it than during the first few days. For instance, the ill-heated rooms are a curse of English life from which one never escapes. So far as Gert is concerned, he doesn't mind the cold much, does he? Probably you will soon be going to see George [the Bishop of Chichester] too. His wife can speak a little German. In view of the fact that he has many friends, it would surely be well for you not to delay your visit to him for too long. He is also the best person to put you in touch with Sir Walter Moberley. Otherwise I can write to him as well. Only in that case you must first send me his address. Please write to me too about Schröeder*. He is in fact very ill with *paralysis agitans* [Parkinson's disease], but perhaps he can still receive you. He was always very kind and helpful to me. I will write first if you want to introduce yourselves, but in that case please let me know. I would of course be very glad to do this, it is only that I would rather not do it if there is no need or if you feel that it would not be of any use. And perhaps your time is already fully occu-pied. Please let me know if you think I can help in any other way. I think of you often every day and wish you every happiness.

With my love,

Yours, Dietrich

A further development was that Gert's younger brother, Peter, who was both able and hardworking, had to hand over into 'Aryan hands' the textile factories at Sommerfeld which he had inherited from his father. He was still in Berlin at this time and we were very anxious about him. But he was able to take refuge with some foreign acquaintances in Berlin and in this way the Gestapo lost track of him. He hastened his arrangements for leaving Germany and was soon with us in London. From there he decided to emigrate to Australia. His courageous Swiss wife

* Baron Schröder, German banker in London.

had already come to London ahead of him for the birth of her first child because they wanted the child to be 'British born' when it entered the world.

In spite of the restricted opportunities for emigration, a brutal pressure was now brought to bear upon those Jews who were still living in Germany to force them to leave, and hence a new stream of refugees arrived in London. As an instance of what was taking place as a result of the oppression and suffering created by the Nazi power in its crudity and malevolence, I may quote from the following letter by Paula Rosenstock. It was written after the Nazis had, in her eightieth year, thrown her out of her home and threatened her with the concentration camp. Paula Rosenstock was the mother of seven children and was no longer willing to leave Germany. She wrote to her children as follows :

My dear children,

I feel that physically and spiritually there is no longer any future for me at this terrible time, and that it is better for us all for me quietly to depart from you and from this earthly life. Do not be sad that I am going home, but continue to work bravely and resolutely at shaping life's course. Remain true to the moral and spiritual aims for which you are striving. Do not let yourselves be blinded by lies and selfishness. May my blessing rest upon you and those who come after you. Give my greetings to all those who think of me with love and friendship. My greetings and blessings to my children and all who come after them, brothers and sisters and friends.

From your grandmother, Paula Rosenstock

The following prayer, composed by Pope John XXIII before his death on 3rd June 1963, seems to have a special relevance here :

'We realize now that for many many centuries blindness has covered our eyes so that we no longer see the beauty of his chosen people and no longer recognize in the faces of that people the features of our own first-born brother. We realize that the mark of Cain is upon our brow. For whole centuries Abel has been lying in blood and tears because we have forgotten your love. Forgive us the curses which we have uttered so unjustly against the Jews. Forgive us for having, in their flesh, crucified you a second time. For we knew not what we did.'

Hans Leibholz, Gert's eldest brother, had already left Germany for Holland a few years before us together with his wife, and he had actually attuned himself to the life there to some extent. He still had his fine furniture which he had been able to take with him, together with the library which he had collected with such care and deep understanding, for he was a great bibliophile. He had been a judge in Berlin. Now in Holland he was no longer engaged in legal work but had found a post in business which entailed frequent journeys to and from London.

We were seeing much of Gert's brothers. One never knew how often circumstances in the future would still make it possible for us to be together. After the Germans had invaded Holland at the end of May 1940 many men of Jewish origin were forcibly transported to concentration camps as far away as Poland. At that time my brother-in-law, Hans Leibholz, took his own life together with his 'Aryan' wife, once so full of zest for living. Neither of them had the strength to continue any longer or to endure the tortures of a concentration camp. They must have spent terrible days and agonizing hours before arriving at this decision.

We refused to accept the designation 'emigrants' as applied to us by the Hitler government because it had an undertone of discrimination. To the English and ourselves we were known as 'refugees'. In his poem 'About the term Emigrants' Bertolt Brecht conveys the difference between the two expressions very well:

I always felt that that name was false
By which we were called, 'Emigrants'.
For that means those who leave of their own accord.
Now we never left of our own accord,
Freely deciding to choose another land.
Nor did we choose to enter any land
So as to settle there
If possible forever.

Rather we fled.

We were driven out, banished.
And the country that received us
Could never be a home,
Only a place of exile.
So we wait restlessly
As close to the borders as we can,
Waiting for the day of our return,
Watching for every tiny change
That takes place over the border,
Eagerly questioning every new arrival,
Forgetting nothing,
Never giving up hope,
Never forgiving, either, what has been done,
Never forgiving.

Ah, the quietness of the hours does not deceive us!
We hear the cries from their camps...
Reaching even this far.
We ourselves are almost like rumours
Of crimes committed there,
Rumours which have drifted over the borders,
Each of us, as he makes his way through the throng
With broken shoes,
Bears witness to the shame
Which now defiles our land.
Yet none of us will remain here.
The last word has not yet been spoken.

England relieved our souls. It was as though a crushing weight fell away: the anxiety for the lives of my husband and children. This is something which we can never forget. All the discomforts which were entailed in our day-to-day lives, financial restrictions, cold, cramped quarters, the loss of our house, our car and our servants—certainly we did feel all this, but it seemed quite small and unimportant. My thoughts hardly ever turned back to my house and furniture. I must admit, however, that some years later when our daughters were growing up I did feel rather differently about this, for then we had to put up with so much ugliness in the furnished lodgings in which we had to live that I often feared that our daughters would never again have

7. Dietrich in the garden at Friedrichsbrunn, aged sixteen

8. The Bonhoeffers' house in the Wangenheimstrasse in Berlin

9. Dietrich as a student aged nineteen

10. Klaus Bonhoeffer in his thirties

11. Dietrich in 1936

any opportunity to acquire an eye for beauty in household things. The saying that in a great misfortune 'one's heart is reconciled in the end, but what hurts is having to do without the little adornments of life' was brought home to me then. But at this early stage our minds were completely occupied with our new life.

Meanwhile, over in Germany my Aunt Elizabeth von Hase was guarding the house together with our cook. We had no intention of selling it. Our bookseller, Robert Schmidt, who was also an opponent of the Hitler régime, was extremely helpful and sent large parcels of books from our library to England. One day he even sent a chest, adding to its contents my violin, which my aunt had given him. Music played a major part in her life and the idea that I was parted from my violin seemed to her something that I would not be able to endure. In reality I had long ceased to play it. But to put it briefly this violin was the spark that set off a major conflagration, for the chest was sent by a route which led through the customs, something that Herr Schmidt had not reckoned with, and it attracted the attention of the customs detectives.

The door was opened by old Lina, who had already had some experience of the persecution of Jews from her previous place. Now she came running to my aunt with her hands in the air crying, 'They're coming, they're coming!', which was not exactly the cleverest thing to do. My aunt was tall, stately and 'Aryan', and at almost sixty-seven years old she still wore her fair hair in two plaits wound round her head. Now she retained her quiet dignity, abashed the 'masters' who entered with such a domineering attitude, and put them 'in their place'. However they then began the process of questioning my aunt and the cook, of sniffing and fingering the contents of the house. The men searched the entire house through. A picture of me was still standing on my husband's desk in which I was wearing a pearl necklace, an old family heirloom. Immediately the official became aggressive and snarled out, 'Where is the Jewess's jewelry?'

To this my aunt replied, 'First my niece is not a Jewess and second I suppose that she has her pearl necklace round her neck where she always wears it.'

Next the Gestapo men demanded to inspect even the guest-room where my aunt was sleeping. Now my aunt had already

E

taken certain books which had been condemned by the Nazis out of the library, and hidden them in her room. She had also just been reading some of the Letters of Rosa Luxemburg. She had only had time hastily to thrust these under her pillow in the mistaken idea that the 'masters' would not sniff it out there. Of course they tracked the book down and pronounced their judgement upon it, as also upon 'aristocrats of this type' who 'read books of this type'. They would soon be on the tracks of these! My aunt was now subjected to eight days of house arrest. After this investigation the Nazis blocked our German bank accounts.

My relatives were afraid that unless a watch was kept on our property in Göttingen it might perhaps be stolen, plundered or confiscated. Because of this the more valuable objects, and among them our grand piano, were taken into the home of a lawyer friend of ours in Berlin, where they were later destroyed by the bombing. Some of our valuables which we had given to our parents were seized by the Russians in 1945 either from their safe or from the estate of Frau von Kleist, where one had at first thought that they would be secure. Some things were left in Göttingen in a warehouse. One of the few bombs which fell in Göttingen blew the roof off so that the rain could stream in. Books were reduced to pulp and only some furniture was still usable, but by then I no longer counted on any of it surviving at all.

In England in 1938 when the season of Advent came round the thought of my children, with whom we had always celebrated this season, and of my parents and brothers and sisters in Germany, as also of our position which still seemed so utterly without prospects, made me very homesick. On one occasion when a well-meaning English lady played me some German Christmas carols on the gramophone, I was overcome at hearing them again. But for this I reproached myself. At the same time, however, we did feel an overpowering longing for woods and beautiful paths, for forest glades and the smell of trees and earth.

A little before Christmas our parents brought our daughters to Holland. Their care for the children on the journey was touching, and to prepare for their departure from Germany they had filled all their trunks with clothes which would 'allow for growing', as my mother put it. Both my parents looked tired. We had wonderful clear winter days in Haarlem and we cele-

brated Christmas at an enchanting house belonging to a cousin
of my mother's. There once more the grown-ups sang German
Christmas carols with all the children on the fourth Sunday in
Advent. My parents could only stay for ten days, but we all
made the best of them. I went with my father to the Franz Hals
Museum, and we also saw the Brueghels, my father taking a
special interest in the Flemish physiognomy as shown on these
pictures. We walked on foot through the city. The wind blew
sharp but this icy cold had a charm of its own. When we saw
our parents off we knew for certain that it would be a long time
before we could visit them again in Germany, and that soon
perhaps our parents would be too old to travel or else would be
separated from us by a war. The thought of this made us feel
very sad.

In January 1939 we received an invitation from the Bishop of
Chichester, a close friend of Dietrich's. He invited us to spend a
week-end with him and to bring the children too. The Bishop of
Chichester was fifty-five years old. He had been educated at
Westminster and Oxford and had formerly been an Oxford don.
During the twenties he had been Dean of Canterbury and since
1929 Bishop of Chichester. Later he became a member of the
House of Lords. In his earlier days he had also been engaged in
social work, and had taken special interest in homes for the
working classes. Through his friendship with my brother he had
become better informed than anyone else in England about the
Church's struggle in Germany, and he supported the Confessing
Church in her conflict with the Nazi régime. He was a strong
supporter of all movements which promoted the unity of the
Churches and the collaboration of all creeds in international and
social matters.

These were pleasant days. The old palace and the splendid
chapel, the fine garden with its well-kept lawns, the walls over-
grown with creepers, the great high rooms with their open fireplaces where Mrs Bell and the Bishop received us so charmingly —
everything was quite new to us and very interesting.

When tea was brought we were still alone with our hosts in the
drawing-room. The children sang them the first English Christmas
carols they had learned. Evening prayers were held in the chapel
as early as six o'clock, and this, too, made a great impression
upon the children. Afterwards at dinner there were several more

guests. Suddenly I saw before me the face of someone I knew, though it was much altered. It was an acquaintance of my younger days, a neighbour during my early childhood, the son of a lawyer from the Grunewald who had subsequently become a lawyer himself. His head was shaved completely bald and he had just been released from a Nazi concentration camp with a warning not to tell what had happened to him—and here he was, still afraid to talk because of the warning, although he was now in Chichester! Of course we had much news to exchange. He intended to go still further and emigrate to the United States with his wife and children.

Dinner took place at a long and wonderful table with well-trained servants to attend to our needs. After this we re-assembled in the drawing-room, where 'Antony and Cleopatra' was read, the various parts being distributed among the company. The beauty of the English language, which is so often contested in Germany, overwhelmed me.

Next morning at seven o'clock a housemaid knocked and brought us two pretty trays from which emanated a wonderful aroma of morning tea. Intending to offer us biscuits, she opened the biscuit-box that stood on our bedside table. We had not realized the purpose of this pretty box, and, to our shame, had already eaten the biscuits the evening before as a 'bedtime snack'. So she departed in astonishment in order to replenish the box, brought us our shoes, drew back the curtains, and wished us 'good morning'. After morning service in the chapel, breakfast was prepared. The Bishop himself handed us our plates of porridge and cream, and later bacon and eggs which had been placed hot on the sideboard. Mrs Bell poured out the tea, a maid brought fresh hot toast and orange marmalade. A huge log fire was blazing in the largest fireplace which I ever saw in England, but even so it was rather cold in that gigantic old dining hall. The conversation turned upon the struggle of the Church, ecumenism, and the problem of finding posts for the refugee pastors.

At the beginning of 1939 an increasing number of voices in England were raised against Chamberlain's policy of appeasement. On every side we heard accusations in which he was made responsible for the fact that Hitler was coming forward with ever-fresh demands, and it was not only among the supporters of Labour that great hostility now prevailed against his policies. Mr

Chamberlain was undoubtedly an *anima candida*, upright and tolerant, a gentleman who could not imagine that Hitler could play him such an underhand trick as to break his word to him. 'This time he gave his promise to *me*', he rejoined to one who doubted Hitler's word. This story was told to me in London at the time. But men had been roused to wakefulness, and were no longer willing to allow themselves to be beguiled. One day posters were suddenly put up along the street and on the hoardings which said 'We have got to be prepared'. We thought that too and were only surprised that there was so little preparation to be seen.

In March 1939 we received a visit from Adam von Trott zu Solz, who had very good connections with British politicians and writers, for instance, Lord Lothian and Lionel Curtis. He tried to warn them of Hitler's expansionist plans and recommended resolute resistance to him. For some time Gert had been troubled with a trigemonal neuralgia which had followed upon a bout of influenza. In consequence our political discussions took place at his bedside. Later he met Trott once more at the house of an English lawyer friend. The majority of the Conservatives still would not allow their confidence in the appeasement policy to be shaken and persisted in labouring under the delusion that this was the way in which peace could best be assured. I often heard it said of Hitler, 'Oh, his bark is worse than his bite'.

Another hope which I often heard expressed was that Hitler would serve as a vanguard against Socialism and Communism. Many had their eyes opened too late and then only when the treaty was signed between Soviet Russia and Germany. Hitler's protestations of peace had lulled so many of the English to sleep.

During September 1938 Dietrich had continued to write his *Life Together* at our house at Göttingen, and now he sent us this 'offspring' of his with the greeting, 'This for the time being; I will follow soon'. Soon after this he sent us Gertrud von Le Fort's book, *The Last One at the Scaffold*. On the first page Dietrich had written, 'I know', which depressed me very much. But I did not have any further opportunity to speak with him about it.

For a long time now we had greatly been looking forward to Dietrich's visit. He had hoped to celebrate our common birthday with me in England, but this was not to be. So he wrote to us in London:

1st February 1939

Dear Sabine,

I am thinking of you and all your family particularly in these days, and would love to hold the celebration with you. So many times in the past we have made plans to celebrate our birthday together once more. Now everything has become so different. Recently it occurred to me that in the research that has been done into twins some kind of laws have been discovered (only I am afraid that they do not really apply to us as we aren't identical twins) to the effect that certain sets of twins often have the same experiences in their lives even though they are living far apart from one another. I must say that to a certain extent this does seem to be in accordance with what we have found, at any rate when we compare ourselves with our brothers and sisters. For us, too, things have turned out very differently, at any rate in recent times, from what we once imagined, though this applies to each of us in his or her own way. To this extent we can perhaps have an especially good understanding between us of the present courses which our lives have taken. Ultimately speaking it is in fact one and the same reality which has had so decisive an effect upon our lives and given them this unexpected twist. But however this may be, at any rate we will be thinking of one another very much on the 4th and promising one another not so much all kinds of good wishes as real mutual support.

Well, I already feel very happy at the prospect of seeing you again. The children will help you to celebrate the 4th beautifully and cheerfully. Together with Eberhard Bethge I am sending you the Ludwig Richter book which you and the children may enjoy. It is a piece from the happiness of the past which we ought to preserve.... I hope it will arrive in time.

My best wishes, then, and love to you all,
With warmest love,

Yours, Dietrich

On the 11th March Dietrich arrived. He brought with him from his Preachers' Seminary at Finkenwalde Eberhard Bethge, his student and friend, whom we already knew and greatly liked. It was as if we were suddenly upheld by someone. Gert and I both felt a great inrush of strength and courage. So much happiness emanated from Dietrich's strong personality, although in fact the times were far from being bright. Certainly I have often seen Dietrich sad. But I never saw him sullen or morose. There were people who said that the sun rose when he entered the room. He was able to be so unreservedly joyful.

Now he wanted to show us a great deal of London. The children, too, had to come with us, and I have happy memories of all kinds of adventures such as excursions to Hampton Court, Kew Gardens, visits to St Paul's, the Tower and Buckingham Palace, as well as to the films, and much else besides; but above all there were visits from old friends. As Dietrich had worked for one and a half years as pastor in the German communities of St Paul's and Sydenham in London, he knew far more of England and English life than we did.

The English spring of 1939 was magical. Forest Hill, next to Sydenham, is situated on higher ground, and from there fine views are to be had, especially over London at evening. It is an old residential area and even as early as this we could sit together in Miss Sharp's garden or play ball with the children. Dietrich lost no time in showing us how to play darts, teaching us to throw the feathered arrows at a target. All his life he greatly enjoyed games in which all could share. Once the children were in bed, he would go upstairs to them and sing them the hymn which runs, 'May all who hate you come to nothing, those who trust to their strength alone'. He also drew the attention of the children to the verses from the hymn *Herzliebster Jesu* which are not sung in the Matthew Passion :

> *I will bear all in your honour,*
> *Neglect no cross, no insult or vexation,*
> *And take no persecution or mortal pain to heart.*
>
> *Lord Jesus then when there before your throne,*
> *The crown of glory is laid upon my head,*
> *Then will I sing my praise and thanks to you.*

Together with Dietrich and the children we had just heard the

Matthew Passion in London. Dietrich also taught the children the
hymn which runs:

> *Follow me, says Christ our hero.*
> *Follow me, you Christians all!*
> *Deny yourselves! Leave the world,*
> *Follow my call as it resounds!*
> *Take your cross and trouble on you,*
> *Follow me wherever I go.*
>
> *If it seems too hard for you,*
> *It is I that go before,*
> *It is I that stand beside you,*
> *I myself, your fellow warrior,*
> *I myself who paves the way,*
> *In the strife it is I who am all.*
>
> *One perhaps may flag in virtue*
> *And seek to tarry. Let him then*
> *Raise his eyes to where his captain*
> *Still advances on before.*

Later we sang this song after Dietrich's final sermon to his
old London community in the church at Sydenham, which is
today called the 'Dietrich Bonhoeffer Church'. Pastor Boeckheler
and his capable warm-hearted sister showed us much kindness. At
that time he was the pastor of the German communities of St
Paul's and Sydenham. On Sundays they often invited us to
lunch. In his pastor's house there were still some pieces of
furniture belonging to my brother, which made me feel very
much at home. We made many visits there in company with
Dietrich too. And on such occasions Dietrich usually sat straight
down at the piano and began to play. Our German palates
delighted in the Swabian dishes which Pastor Boeckheler's sister
served. Pastor Julius Rieger, a friend of Dietrich's from his London
days, also showed himself an extremely sensitive and helpful
friend to the German refugees, and his wife, who was always
so hard-working, was also touching in her solicitude for the
welfare of refugees and helped where she could, even though she
herself had a large family to provide for.

In those weeks in London we all discussed with Dietrich what he should do for the best in case he was called to the German forces. The Confessing Church had not defined its attitude towards conscription, and Dietrich's thoughts hovered between leaving the country, serving in the missions, or entering the Army Medical Service. To take up weapons in Hitler's war was for him simply out of the question. He was not prepared to take part in any other way than in joining the medical service. I can still see him writing to the Bishop of Chichester in order to ask his advice. He also consulted his American friends.

On the 15th March we heard on the radio that Hacha, the President of Czechoslovakia, had been placed under such strong pressure by Hitler that he had signed the treaty for a German protectorate over Bohemia and Moravia. The moment this was signed the German motorized columns drove into Czechoslovakia. On the 16th March any trust that the world had had in Hitler's word was finally exhausted. Only one week later Hitler was applying pressure on the Poles to return Danzig, and the B.B.C. brought news of a partial mobilization in the Polish Corridor and also of the rejection of Hitler's demands. On the day following this we heard of Hitler's invasion of the Memel Province.

In spite of everything, spring was coming in full force. The forsythia and the dark mauve lilacs bloomed enchantingly and luxuriantly in the old gardens of Forest Hill, and the daffodils gleamed from the broad expanses of the parks, stirred by a restless spring breeze.

Soon strong and angry criticisms of the appeasement policy began once more to make themselves heard. Chamberlain now announced in a speech which he made at Birmingham that there would be no more of it. To us it seemed extremely late in the day for this. On the 27th April, England introduced general conscription. Many took this as a serious sign, and the people in London were very depressed. Throughout all this disquieting news everyday life continued. Dietrich visited old members of the community and enjoyed being in England again and showing it to his friend, Eberhard Bethge. Many old acquaintances of Dietrich's wanted to see him again, and Dietrich wanted to introduce us everywhere.

On one occasion we went into London to see a film. During the film Dietrich wanted to light a cigarette. But as he struck a match in the dark the whole box caught fire. Although the flame flared up quickly he simply held the box in the palm of his hand until he could tread out the fire on the floor without danger to anyone. He now had a great burn over the whole palm of his hand.

At that time Dietrich regarded our accommodation at Miss Sharp's as inadequate in the extreme, and considered that we would 'soon have to find somewhere decent of our own to live'. Admittedly he was an optimist with regard to the prospects of obtaining professional work in England for a professor of German constitutional law. In fact it was only those working in the field of the natural sciences who had a certain right to optimism of this kind. Even established heads of hospitals were obliged to take their medical examinations again in England and America. We had to cut our coat according to the cloth. Thus for the time being we did not contemplate any change. I am still aware of how awful Dietrich found our room, though in fact it seemed quite comfortable to us even if it was very different from what we had been used to.

One morning Dietrich suggested a visit to the Caledonian Market. It seemed quite unique to me, this mixture of junk and antique stalls in an open market-place. Here he picked up for five pounds an Indian divan cover made out of blue cloth and embroidered with gold thread, 'so that you have at least one beautiful thing to look at in your room'. His friend, Eberhard Bethge, would have liked to buy a wind instrument, but to this Dietrich objected, saying that in England money should be spent only on us refugees. The currency allowance for German visitors was very meagre.

A place where one could always count on meeting a few interested English people as well as German and Austrian refugees from the Nazis was Hans Preiss's bookshop near the British Museum. This was another place which we used to visit with Dietrich. Here one could read or discuss politics, and refugees took their own books there to be sold. It was an excellent bookshop. The owner was himself a refugee and had a burning interest in politics. Pastor Rieger and Pastor Büsing were often to be seen here too, and refugees who had been working in the British Museum liked to look in at Preiss's on their way home.

Sometimes we used to go on from here to have lunch together

at Lyons or, on more festive occasions, even at the Schmidt Restaurant for a German lunch. On these occasions it was often Pastor Rieger who kindly acted as host. Baron Schröder, the London banker, gave him many a cheque to relieve the serious financial straits in which the refugees found themselves. Often conditions became particularly catastrophic when in addition to all their other difficulties they fell sick, for at that time there was no adequate health service and the doctors' fees were very high. Here, too, Hitlerism made them feel its cruel after-effects, for many found that no other course was open to them than to treat their illness by themselves or to ignore it and struggle on as best they might.

When Dietrich and Eberhard Bethge returned to Germany once more we could still hope that it would not be long before a further meeting with them in London could be arranged. Dietrich had just been to see Professor Niebuhr, the Director of the Union Theological Seminary in New York, who was in England having a period of rest on the south coast. Dietrich discussed his situation with Niebuhr and asked him whether he could give some lectures in New York. He also let it be seen that in the event of war breaking out he would if possible remain there. We were still waiting for an answer to this, but Niebuhr had immediately sent a telegram to set the matter in motion in the United States on Dietrich's behalf. This made it easier to say good-bye.

So far we had never had any financial worries during our twelve years of married life, but now every penny mattered. The money which we had been able to bring out in 1937-8 amounted to only five per cent of our capital. Whereas those who emigrated in 1933 had still been able to take their capital with them, after 1938 the refugees from Hitler's persecution, among them thousands of children, came over with ten marks in their pockets and imposed a heavy burden on the refugee committees, the more so since at first they could not obtain any work permits. In Germany any attempt to transfer money abroad illegally was punishable with penal servitude, and in the case of Jews and 'non-Aryans' this meant, in practice, concentration camp and death. Between 1938 and 1940 alone about twenty thousand children came to England. Many households opened their doors to the refugee children. In these, conditions varied very greatly, but they were often received with great love and the English families often made great sacrifices on behalf of their refugee children. To us, too, many acts of kindness were shown and offers of help were made, and later we also experienced true friendship. We had much to learn that was new. I found that English women took a far more active part in public affairs. Even women with little education took an interest in books, though these might be no more than the novels and travel books which they borrowed from the city libraries. For instance they knew the name of their member of parliament and sometimes they also knew him personally as a result of house-to-house visiting and they read about him in their newspaper. But their standards in household matters were lower than what was customary in Germany. The struggle against the coal dust in London seemed to have been given up. The curtains that hung before the dusty windows were deeply begrimed, and in the underground stations and trains the raincoats the passengers wore to protect their clothing were very grubby. On one occasion I saw a woman of the lower middle classes serving her husband's evening meal on a newspaper on the kitchen table, probably in order to save the trouble of washing up. But in simple households I also saw kitchen tables covered with clean oil-cloth and laid with the utmost care for husband and children. On the whole, however, the rooms were far less well cared for than in corresponding households in Germany. Admittedly the upper classes lived in the most beautiful houses with splendid furniture, old pictures, enchanting gardens and everything looked after by a staff of good servants.

What hours of discussion we spent in the effort of trying to penetrate the British character! I love the English and have deep trust in them in spite of the criticisms which I have made and will make at various points in this book.

It always struck me how attentively people listened, especially when a lady had something to say, and this was in sharp contrast to the habits of many German men, who will often not allow a lady so much as a single word, not infrequently interrupt her, sometimes tease her, and frequently deliver long, instructive monologues at her without finding out first if she wishes to hear them. An English gentleman never behaves in such a way as to make his companion feel more stupid, socially inferior, less important or unsure of himself. He shows this modesty and politeness to women too. In the mornings even though the expression on the Englishman's features may not be precisely one of enjoyment, still he covers over his lack of enthusiasm by giving an amiable greeting in the form of some small hopeful remark about the weather: 'Isn't it a fine day today?' or 'Not so bright this morning but perhaps it will clear up later'. I never failed to find such remarks a little disarming. Further I was interested to notice that in England people avoid burdening each other with accounts of their physical condition. Illness is hardly ever spoken of. It is not a fit subject for discussion. Feeling sorry for oneself is an attitude which the English abhor, and it seemed to be actually more correct to be ignorant about the organic processes of one's own body.

Schadenfreude, or gloating over another's misfortune, is an attitude which I never experienced. It is significant that there is no word for this in English. I found that a man would often speak of his failures, never of his successes. It was far simpler than is supposed to live on good terms with English people. It took little trouble to understand their wishes, and the key to all relationships was mutual consideration. A certain distance was maintained between individuals, since 'familiarity breeds contempt' and this applied to almost all human relationships. Reason rather than emotion prevails, and one never exacerbates an emotional situation. It struck me how obliging and gentle the English are. Admittedly one has to adopt certain specific patterns of behaviour. One should never be interfering and should occupy oneself solely with one's own affairs. There were postcards bearing the words 'Do someone a good turn every day—leave them alone!'. One must not take oneself too seriously or show too adoring an attitude towards one's children or spoil them. Everyday we discovered something new about England. Always on leaving the bathroom or lavatory one should leave the door a little ajar. If the door is left closed this of itself is a way of saying 'occupied', and no-one will turn the handle from outside. Only refugees and other foreigners would do this by mistake—to the confusion of those inside. Such minor mishaps confirmed the English in their conviction that 'all foreigners are a little mad'.

I found that the English are touchingly grateful for little pleasures that one devises for them. Indeed there is something absolutely childlike about their gratitude. On the other hand the attitude of the English towards gifts is somewhat cold and conventional, Christmas, for example, being the supreme occasion for such unimaginative gifts as calendars, engagement books, and items from the chemist's.

Soon we began to derive great amusement from *Punch*, a periodical which we had never before been able to understand. The self-criticism of the English as, for instance, when they depict their tendency towards *laissez-faire* or their reluctance to throw anything away or a certain proneness to find things today changed for the worse in comparison with the old days, their readiness to procrastinate—the humorous periodicals have their own quite special way of illustrating all this, and in general English humour is something quite unique. This applies to the political jokes too. Our English acquaintances were quite unable to see the humour of Wilhelm Busch. They found him lacking in subtlety. This lack of subtlety was ascribed to the Germans in general though they were also credited with a certain openness and straightforwardness and with great ability. But then it was precisely not regarded as over-endearing to have quite so much ability.

We soon lost the habit of attempting to shake hands when greeting someone in the morning. Once one finds that one's hand meets nothing but empty air when one extends it one learns one's lesson. In the morning when we came down to breakfast we used to say 'good morning' as we entered the room, only to find the other boarding-house guests for the most part deep in their newspapers. Each one would first read his own and then exchange it for someone else's. Hardly a word was spoken. My husband, the children and I had a table to ourselves where we had breakfast very cosily together and conversed with one another in undertones—though from politeness only in English. Once we were outside we could hear so many other languages in the London streets that we could confidently talk German with one another. I still have pleasant memories of the smell of warm toast on those early mornings. Breakfast in these circumstances was a most pleasant occasion and one which my brother Dietrich, too, particularly enjoyed experiencing again when he visited us in March. He understood so well how to enjoy this to the full. To those who really want to eat well in England, Somerset Maugham makes the suggestion that they should have three breakfasts brought to them.

In the meantime Dietrich's American friends had sent him the expected invitation to New York to give a series of lectures at the Union Theological Seminary, and on the 3rd June 1939 he came to us in London shortly before his departure for America. There was much to talk about and he also wanted to have a little more time with our children.

In those June days of 1939 it was as though people coming abroad from Germany wanted to take one last breath of fresh air before a new crisis or a war befell them. My eldest brother, Karl-Friedrich Bonhoeffer, also visited us on the way to the United States and spent a few days more with us in London. These were pleasant times, though admittedly not free from anxieties for the future. Karl-Friedrich had been offered a professorship at the University of Chicago and he wanted to obtain a closer view of conditions there. He knew the States and later made the journey there with Dietrich. But he soon returned. He could not make up his mind in these uncertain times to leave his parents behind in Germany. On his way to the U.S. Dietrich wrote from the 'Bremen' on 20th June 1939:

Dear Sabine,
   We will land in a few hours. The crossing was smooth. I found the keys at once in the leather suitcase. Did you get the telegram? How did Gert's visit in Oxford go? Let me know about it soon. I expect I will hear today what they intend to do with me. Keep well, we will be writing to each other often.
                    Love to you all,
                                        Dietrich

The prospect of knowing that Dietrich was in the States, so that we could at any rate always write to one another, was a saving grace. In case of war he would have found a place of refuge and could have paved the way for us, too, to go to the States if an invasion had taken place. Thus their departure was not without consolation for us when both brothers set sail for the United States. It was typical of Dietrich that he would not forget his god-child's birthday even in those hectic days. He wrote from New York,

June 24, 1939

Dear Marianne,

I hope this card will reach you punctually on your birthday. I wish you many happy returns and a happy day and a good new year, in which I hope you will see many new and interesting and lovely things and in which I hope you will give your parents pleasure every day. Here it is also quite nice and interesting and perhaps you will all be travelling here one day. But I think where you are now it is really still nicer. The skyscrapers you see on this card aren't even the highest. There is one that is 360 metres high, higher than the Hexentanzplatz* by Bode. Now give my love to your parents, Miss Sharp, Miss Witte, and Christiane. Very much love and very best wishes,

Your Uncle Dietrich

At the end of June a card arrived for us from Dietrich:

New York, June 1939

In view of the terrible situation over there, and since I would in any case have remained here only until August, I have decided to return sooner with Karl-Friedrich. Accordingly I will be in Southampton on the 13th July unless things take a sudden change for the better. I cannot give you any idea how long I shall be able to remain with you in London. We must see. Perhaps only for a short time.

With warmest love,

Yours, Dietrich

On the 13th July 1939 Dietrich came to us in London and we had him with us until the 25th July. It was to be the last time. He knew that war was on the point of breaking out and was full of anxiety for his young pastors. And he said that he had suddenly felt it impossible to remain in the United States. Certainly his American friends had shown the utmost kindness, doing everything in their power to keep him over there in order to provide for his safety. He had been offered a professorship and also a post as pastor to the refugees. But these would be able to

* Hexentanzplatz, 'witches' dancing place', is a place near Friedrichsbrunn where Dietrich went as a child.

do without him and he might even be depriving one of them of this post as pastor. There he could perfectly well be replaced, whereas in Germany there was need of him. He could not leave his young theologians, his brethren, in the lurch in this difficult crisis of conscience to which the war would now expose them. He must return.

We were very shocked. What would be the outcome of this? Was it madness? Did it have to be? But by now Dietrich was so utterly convinced that it did have to be, and he was free, secure and seemed unburdened. We hardly dared to suggest any possible objections in the face of such determination. Moreover I, too, could well understand his feeling that during the war he did not want to be somewhere where his parents, brothers, sisters and friends could not reach him, and where he was incapable of standing by them. With him, the desire to maintain close and living ties with his parents and his young theologians was very strong. All three of us knew what his return to Germany would mean for us, and this was an aspect of the matter that we hardly touched upon in our discussions.

Dietrich was sitting at the piano and singing with the children, when Pastor Rieger entered in a state of great shock and brought him the terrible news of the death of Pastor Paul Schneider in the concentration camp at Buchenwald. Dietrich was very pale as he told us of this. I remember that he had difficulty with his breathing and that he turned to the children and said, 'Listen carefully, children. This is a name which you must never forget. Paul Schneider is our first martyr.' Then he told them about him.

As early as 1932 Dietrich had on one occasion preached a sermon on the fact that the blood of martyrs would once more be demanded: 'But even if we really have courage and faith enough to shed this blood then, it will still be neither so innocent nor so eloquent as that of the first witnesses. Our blood would be tainted with a great personal sin: the sin of the unprofitable servant.'

On the 25th July Dietrich departed from us. Shortly before, he came in with some of his clothes over his arms, his dressing-gown, his panama hat, ties, scarves, pyjamas, 'so that we should have a few more things in England'. We all accompanied Dietrich to the station. It was a grave parting. In his own way, optimistic and self-controlled as ever, Dietrich helped us through it. But we had all seen the storm signals ahead and had not much hope of seeing each other again very soon.

I never saw Dietrich again.

In spite of the intensification of the crisis, our parents gave us great joy by paying one more visit to Holland towards the end of July 1939 so that we might see one another again before it was too late. We met in August in Zandvoort and spent two unforgettable weeks with them and the children. For all his seventy years, my father still often bathed with us and swam outstandingly well. He would have liked to swim far out to sea with me but he was very considerate and did not want to cause my mother anxiety. This was always uppermost in his mind. He hated people to be made anxious and must have regarded it as very unhealthy. I will never forget one occasion when Gert had been travelling by car and arrived late for a meal. The moment he saw him my father greeted him with the words, 'Your wife has been waiting for you. She has been anxious'. Nothing further was said but there could be no mistaking the tone in which it was uttered. Otherwise my father never interfered and had a very good relationship with my husband and with all his sons-in-law. He only gave advice when he was asked.

It is striking how vividly I can still remember these days in Holland, and how we enjoyed ourselves, although we firmly believed that war was coming and were deeply anxious as to how Dietrich, as a conscientious objector, would cope with the difficulties he had to face, and we worried as to what lay in store for our other brothers, brothers-in-law and many friends.

But the sea, the sun, the brilliance of it all, the broad sandy shore, still far from being overcrowded at that time, the happy children—it all made this August of 1939 an unforgettable one.

On the 23rd August Hitler signed a non-aggression pact with the Soviet Union. On the 25th August the world heard that England had signed a treaty pledging her support for Poland. According to all the reports that leaked through, Hitler must already have fixed the actual day for the attack. We received one more visit, this time from Gert's assistant at Göttingen who now pressed home with all speed to join his wife and children.

Prompted by the desire not to be in London with the children when war began we decided to go to Hastings. Even as early as this many parents were separating themselves from their children and some even sent them to acquaintances in America. I found that the English are not, basically speaking, very much given to planning ahead. But they are gifted artists at 'muddling through' and improvisation, and this is infectious.

We first went to stay in an hotel not far from the sea and then wanted to look about and find a more permanent place to stay and a good school, of which there were many situated on the south coast. At that time the possibility of an invasion was not yet envisaged whereas the bombing of London certainly was. Some people wondered if the barrage balloons which went up all over London would be of use after all. They looked fantastic, these elephant-like balloons floating in the sky over London.

14

The outbreak of war and internment

The tension increased hourly. On the 1st September Hitler invaded Poland. England and France pointed to their treaty obligations and urged him to withdraw his troops. We waited with intense anxiety for Chamberlain's speech on the 3rd September, for the time limit for the English ultimatum had expired. None of us will ever forget the news Chamberlain brought as we, together with the English guests in the hotel, pressed round the wireless. At 11 o'clock in the morning we heard: 'Great Britain finds herself in a state of war with Germany'. At five o'clock in the afternoon France, too, declared that she stood by her pact with Poland and was therefore at war with Germany.

An old lady who was listening to the declaration of war—she had spent seventeen years working for lepers in the dominions together with her husband, a minister—said, 'Now we can only pray'. She had let her flat to us, and on this 3rd September we had straightaway to transfer ourselves to this although our heads were reeling after the news. The manager of the hotel told us with great kindness that we should not think that now, because of the declaration of war, we had to leave. They would be glad for us to stay. For financial reasons, however, this was quite out of the question. Just as I was making my way to our new home through the street with a heap of clothes over my arm the sirens sounded. Up till then I had only heard that wailing sound during the trial alarms in Germany. Now it sounded dreadful. The window of our bedroom opened southwards onto the sea and all the morning through we could see ships from the

English fleet moving on the horizon, looking wonderfully white
and gleaming in the sun. We proceeded with the unpacking of
the trunks as in a dream. The inner tension we felt was terrible.
At that time I made a vow to myself never to forget that England
had absolutely never wanted this war. At the stations, in the
shops, and in our own house we heard many English people
speaking about this. Not one of them wanted the war, neither
the men nor the women, the old nor the young. The churches
were full to bursting. England was praying for peace. I can still
hear the whole church singing and the refrain 'We beseech thee
O Lord, hear our prayer'. It made a tremendous impression on me.
Once Chamberlain had told the people clearly that England had
to stand by the treaty of assistance to Poland and that Poland
had been invaded by Hitler one heard it said again and again,
'We must stand by our word of honour'. In practice, the English
were unable to give any further help to Poland and many
English people were distressed by this. In England the majority
could still be appealed to in the name of decency, fairness,
tolerance and even religion.

About the outbreak of the Second World War in Germany my
father wrote as follows:

'The mood in which the German people entered the war in
1939 was radically different from that of 1914.... In 1939 the
population had no doubt that what they were faced with was
a war of aggression prepared and organized by Hitler, and for
this the majority had no sympathy whatever. During the years
from 1933 to the war itself one had got to know the Party, with
its attitude of hostility towards every expression of free opinion.
As a result one was compelled to fear that if Hitler and his
faction were victorious the hubris of the Party would know
no bounds, whereas if they were defeated this would mean the
destruction and impoverishment of Germany. Not a few held
that of these alternatives a victory for Hitler would constitute
the greater danger to European civilization. It was almost
impossible to find any real eagerness to fight for such a victory
except among the young soldiers, young men who had been
through the Hitler Youth. Of course the younger generation
itself was already completely under the power of the terror
which Hitler had created. After the war had flared up the

situation for many, even for such as were hostile to Hitler, became one in which they were fighting for the defence of their homeland. Many a one consoled himself with the hope that in case of victory Hitler would decide upon a more moderate form of government. Of course their hopes for a change of heart of this kind were, given Hitler's character, virtually without foundation.'

In those first months of the war, then, we set up home at St Leonards-on-Sea. Here I had to learn to run my home on thoroughly English lines, and this began straightaway with the ration book. Neither the strange weights and measures nor yet the English money caused me any trouble. I was still young and it was all interesting to me, including the questions which people were discussing in the shops. There was much political talk but although people in the stores knew that I was German I did not feel I was discriminated against. The working-class people even went out of their way to be helpful and pleasant.

At first I rejoiced for all our sakes at the prospect of living by the seaside. It was something I had always wanted. As a child, from the age of ten to fourteen, I had thought of the summer almost exclusively from the standpoint of swimming. Now I wanted the children to have their chance of this. But autumn was already upon us and so we did not manage it. War had broken out and we had other cares. However, there were occasions even in winter when we could sit by the sea with our picnic lunch. There was no sandy beach and only a pebble strand, but still the sun did come out every now and then and the sea did us good. On the promenade a number of benches were set at intervals, shielded from the north and west winds by glass panels. Here the pensioners and old ladies liked to sit in the sun, knitting, reading their papers or discussing politics. Up the hill stretched the London road and here, only five minutes from the sea, was the small old-fashioned furnished flat we had rented. Beyond, the road led up to a residential area of St Leonards with very beautiful and well-tended gardens. Here the Bishop of Chichester had, on his own initiative, rented a large old house where he had given shelter to forty Protestant pastors from Germany together with their families. These had been persecuted by the Nazis because of their Jewish descent. Now they were to be installed by him in course of time in various parishes as curates or vicars. This was all the more difficult for him because the English of many pastors was very poor, but in the case of most of them his tireless efforts eventually succeeded. In the First World War it would have been impossible to give any German pastor a post in an English parish however friendly his dispositions might have been towards England.

The Bishop of Chichester had asked Canon Griffiths to look after the Protestant pastors and their families. Griffiths had a strong sense of humour and could actually laugh at many of the weaknesses of his protégés. A friendly spirit prevailed among them, but still, with so many pastors and their families under a single roof, it was not so easy to cope with all this! Griffiths was probably one of the most likeable ministers whom we came to know in England, being open, cordial and not 'parsonified'. But he did expect everyone to come to his services. From time to time we visited the home for the refugee pastors. Our children liked to play there with the others in the fine old garden, something which we no longer had ourselves.

On the 30th November 1939 the Russians began their attack upon Finland. Old ladies and schoolgirls were now to be seen knitting white balaclava helmets and scarves for the Finnish soldiers fighting in the snow. But when no progress was made in the advance excitement soon died down. The English were astonished that the Finns could hold out against the Russians right until March.

The year 1940 brought one alarm after another. Disregarding the neutrality of Denmark and Norway, Hitler proceeded to occupy those countries. Many took comfort in the fact that the English were laying mines round the Norwegian coasts. The occupation of Narvik by the British forces was cause for celebration. Narvik was held by them up to the beginning of June. In May, King Haakon of Norway arrived in London together with his ministers. He lost no time in forming a government in exile.

In the meantime, however, Hitler had invaded Holland and Belgium and occupied both countries. On the 15th May, Queen Wilhelmina of Holland, together with Crown Princess Juliana and her ministers, arrived in London and likewise formed a government in exile. On the 28th May, Brussels was surrendered without a struggle and the Belgian king had a castle assigned to him in which he could remain. But a group did emerge which likewise formed a government in exile abroad and wanted to continue the struggle.

On the 10th May the attack on France had also begun, and it only took until the 22nd June for the armistice to be signed. De Gaulle came to London and, as leader of all the Free French, called for a resistance. 'France has lost a battle but not the war', he proclaimed. On the 10th June Italy, too, declared war upon both England and France and hoped to be able to share in the booty.

Blow after blow fell. By the end of July 1940 England stood alone. But fortified by the speeches of Churchill she withstood these disasters astonishingly well. At the same time in this precarious situation the attitude towards the German refugees became unmistakably hostile and unfriendly and we avoided speaking German.

In February 1940 the deeds which had been perpetrated in the Warsaw Ghetto became known in England. There was great horror at the brutality of the S.S.

On Whit Monday 1940 we returned home from a walk to Battle to hear from Mrs McDonald, a kind old lady who lived in the flat below, that the police had called and would call again. We guessed what lay ahead of us and soon afterwards a policeman appeared and said it was his duty to take Gert into internment. He patted me consolingly on the shoulder and said, 'Do not distress yourself Madam, he will be back soon. It will take about a week'. Why he had to go and where, he was quite unable to say. There was some quick packing to be done and the children were crying. With my encouragement, Christiane made endless packets of sandwiches for her father and many edibles vanished into Gert's suitcase although the policeman declared that this was quite unnecessary. However these precautions for his future welfare turned out to be extremely valuable.

My heart was heavy but I tried not to show what I felt. Gert was depressed and taken aback but outwardly calm. I knew what was in his mind. At that time he was afraid that England would not stand up to Hitler's invasion, and in that case the refugee camps would be taken over by the S.S. Now the process of living only from day to day began in earnest. It was very hard for us to say good-bye. Nowhere did one any longer feel at home.

All male refugees of German or Austrian nationality between the ages of sixteen and seventy, and even many German women together with their children were now interned. At the police station one policeman remarked spitefully to Gert, 'Now you will have to suffer for your Fuehrer'. My husband replied 'Thank you, I have already done that in Germany'.

On their arrival in England all refugees had already been examined before a tribunal as to their political reliability, and we ourselves had been designated in our passports as 'Refugees from National Socialist Oppression'. In view of this the internment, and the new designation of 'Enemy Aliens', was a blow to us. I, too, packed my trunk and the children's so as to be ready to travel in case we were to be interned. For ten days I remained without news of any kind. My husband was not allowed to write. We had decided that I should remain at St Leonards until I should hear from him, so that each of us would always know where the other was. Now we heard that the German and Austrian refugees were to be transported to Australia and Canada, and I waited longingly for a letter. I found it very difficult to understand why it should be precisely the English, who so passionately championed the cause of freedom for our menfolk, who should have imprisoned them. After all, it was because they had been threatened with loss of freedom that they had been forced to leave their own country. I expressed this disappointment of mine to an English lady, but she only replied in pained tones, 'You must not think badly of England'.

In the meantime, Mr Griffiths, the vicar, visited me repeatedly and wanted to persuade me to leave St Leonards. The piers had already been removed and the landing of the Nazi troops could take place at any time.

'And,' he added gravely, 'You will be shot.'

I replied, 'I would rather remain here with the children until I am once more in contact with my husband by letter and have his address. This is what we have decided'.

Mr Griffiths rejoined, 'None of you will survive this struggle, but you will enter into a better life'.

Then he sat down and we all had tea and he told me of a place he knew in Devon which would be just right for us. The widow of a doctor was living there in a large country house with a glorious garden, and she wanted to take in only German refugees. So there were also English people who still thought like that! I was moved when he then went on to ask, 'Are you in any way short of money?'

When I assured him that I was not he stood up, said a prayer for the release of my husband and for peace, gently pulled Christiane's plaits (he found these especially charming) and disappeared. But soon these plaits had to go because Christiane's schoolfellows started to call after her, 'You are Hitler's daughter! You have sent this beastly aeroplane', and one boy used them as an excuse to torment and annoy Christiane. So I cut them off.

My husband had been taken to the Alien's Internment Camp at Huyton in Liverpool where the conditions were wretched. In these days of unprecedented political tension, newspapers were forbidden there. The uncertainty combined with the embargo on writing or receiving letters was naturally disquieting and depressing in the extreme. Many internees became so deeply depressed that they decided to commit suicide. Some attempted it and some actually succeeded. The prospect of deportation to Australia or Canada was a prime cause of alarm.

On the 3rd July 1940 eleven hundred internees were made to embark for the English Dominions on the *Arandora Star*. They included Germans living abroad who were Nazis together with the refugees from Hitler's persecution and also Italians, both Fascists and anti-Fascists. The *Arandora Star* was torpedoed and sunk by a German U-Boat. About six hundred men were drowned. I heard this news at a time when Gert had written to me to say that he would do all in his power to avoid being transported to the Dominions. These were anxious weeks. In the camps suicides occurred again among the refugees. Many of the wives who were themselves interned could not obtain any information beforehand of whether their husbands or sons would be transported to Australia or Canada. There was an attitude of resentment in the camps. There were always between Nazis and refugees aggressors and victims of outrage, hatred and quarrels, and it was not hard to understand why the inmates should be so implacably opposed to one another. Later the English government decreed that those Germans who had been persecuted on political and racial grounds should be separated from the Nazis.

As soon as the Bishop of Chichester heard that Gert had been interned, he came to St Leonards to visit me. He was distressed to find that the internment laws were being applied to all without distinction. He promised me to do all that lay in his power, and said that he hoped that he would be able to obtain Gert's discharge. Before he took his leave he went down on his knees and prayed aloud for Gert's release from confinement, and also for Dietrich and his brothers. At that time however, conditions were not yet ripe for the liberation of the German refugees who had been interned. After the fall of France and the entry of Italy into the war their position was even worse than before.

We ourselves took the view that someone who stands for the same aims as those for which his host country had entered the war is more than a refugee. He is an ally. There were some truly noble spirits who actively opposed the harassment of the refugees. The Archbishop of Canterbury said, 'The spirit in which we fight is more important than the fact of winning a military victory. If we fell into the Nazi mentality and then won, it would mean the same for the world as if the Nazis won'.

Certain individuals raised the question of the detention of refugees in Parliament although this was just the time at which England was passing through her most perilous hours and the atmosphere was extremely tense. We admired their efforts greatly. The military authorities had demanded the internment in view of the damage which the Fifth Column had caused in Holland and Belgium and the policy of internment was popular. In spite of this, these brave and disinterested men stood up, influenced public opinion, and finally succeeded in changing its direction. Graham White gave expression to the motives which prompted them in the House of Commons: 'The decision which we have to take is not governed by nationalist criteria. We have to draw a distinction between those who are at one with us with regard to certain ideals and those who have different ideals'.

Ten days after the internment of my husband I received my first letter with his address. In order to read it in peace I locked myself in my room with it. It only took me ten minutes to decide to accept Mr Griffiths' offer, and two hours later I was travelling to Devon with the children and the fourteen trunks which contained all our possessions. Griffiths impressed it upon the children that on the way they should not speak a single word of German, and he gave them each half-a-crown for the journey which at the time seemed strange to me but still very touching. It seemed to me right after all to leave St Leonards although we had just found a good school for the girls there, for I had already been asked why I hung my bedclothes out of the window and whether I was trying to give signals to personnel from the German navy. I realized that in England it is not the custom to hang out the bedding like this, probably because of the damp. But on this occasion the sun had been shining and it was so gloriously warm, and the idea never crossed my mind that this could give rise to any suspicion. Again, the washing on the roof garden struck one English lady as suspicious, and from then onwards I exercised extreme caution so as not to give any occasion for mistrust.

The journey to Willand in Devon lasted the entire day. We could see the Home Guard at their work, and many columns of soldiers. The Home Guard were putting up barricades in the streets. The children kept their promise, not a single word of German crossed their lips. Our fourteen trunks were in the luggage van, but we had to change trains three times and each time Marianne, with all of her twelve years, did her utmost to ensure that they were taken out and transferred to the new train on which we had to travel. She was really making every effort to take responsibility and enjoyed it when she was given any; whereas Christiane, who was three and a half years younger, was still completely a child and occupied with her games. She chose the very moment when we were trying to set out on our journey to trouble me with a problem. She complained most energetically that there was a little pencil missing from the pencil box which went with her dolls, so that this could not now be taken with us on our journey.

On our arrival at Willand we were met by a stately and imposing lady in her seventies. She lived in a fine house with a large garden. She herself had had twelve children and her husband had been a well-known doctor. A picture showing all her children in a row was hanging by her desk. Now all her children had long grown up and four of them had already died. She first told me the names of those who had died, pointing a finger at each in turn with the words, 'This one went to God, this one went to God ...', and her voice was filled with the assured conviction that these children were under God's protection. Mrs Wilkinson now lived alone with one old servant. She was a devout and energetic lady who did much good. In the morning she assembled us all for prayers. During prayers she went down on her knees and the rest of us, too, knelt on the hard stone floor. She had taken in other German refugees as well. She showed me into a room furnished with an English double bed and a child's bed. The double bed was for me and my twelve-year-old daughter to sleep in, but I only slept very badly in it, and in general I hated the English double beds, which were too small for two and too big for one. I was glad that my mother could not see the cramped quarters in which we had to live as refugees for so many years. How she would have cast about right and left to try to bring us some help!

I always felt especially sorry for the more elderly among those who had been driven out by Hitler. Often they were no longer in good health and found if very difficult to learn English, for their hearing, too, was failing. Where once they had lived in spacious houses their quarters were now reduced to single rooms where they had to live in very primitive conditions for years at a time.

At Willand I received regular letters from my husband, and my main occupation consisted in writing to various English acquaintances who might be able to help me to secure his release. My husband was very pressing about this and I did all that I could. The internees received only a certain ration of writing paper of a prescribed sort. Later my husband told me that often he would exchange a small piece of sausage (soon I was able to send him certain foodstuffs regularly) with one of his fellow internees for a sheet of writing paper, for many of them did not use their ration of paper. My husband was astonished to see how much more dependent the elderly men often were on the food, which was in any case very bad, and disagreeable scenes took place. When the internees were conducted through the city there were jeers and cries such as '... at last Churchill is doing something'. But it had been relatively simple to take *these* people captive. At that time the English government had not taken the trouble to give any real information to the public about them.

The weeks we spent in Willand were a holiday for the children. Mrs Wilkinson's beautiful house was situated not far from the sea. We admired the Devon countryside, the villages with their thatched and white-washed old cottages, their front gardens full of brightly coloured flowers. There was rich grazing for the sleek-looking cows on the meadows, which were always soft and green. Here nothing went in need. The trees, which were not too thickly grouped and were surmounted by splendid spreading crowns, really did look just as they do in the pictures of the English Romantic painters. It was all very enjoyable to the eye and the summer was quite unusually sunny. There was little forestry cultivation here and broad stretches of the countryside seemed like one great nature reserve. Marianne, our eldest child, was, even at the age of twelve, very interested in the politics of the day, and already had a good understanding of the position of the refugees and the internees. She helped me and together we kept guard on the heavy trunk which contained Gert's manuscripts, among which one article entitled 'Germany between East and West' caused me particular disquiet. On one occasion, Marianne hid this in the oven and on another in the grandfather clock. Finally we secretly buried this trunk in the garden at Willand, for I was afraid that if the Nazis landed and house-to-house searches were instituted these writings could be the cause of Gert being put to death. Soon the first airmen were shot down and then there was great anxiety for it was expected that parachutists, too, would follow. Many rumours were spread about landings allegedly made by these armed combatants, and I remember how one night—for I myself had become infected with this anxiety—I heard a great rustling from the long grass and bushes outside. I went to the window and listened more closely. But when I went down all I discovered was a most homely-looking cow which had wandered into the garden.

Churchill's speech of the 13th May, in which he declared that all he had to offer was 'blood, toil, tears and sweat' had had an effect like a thunderclap. Now all were aroused. On the 22nd June we were listening to the news when the announcement came, 'France has stopped fighting'. At that moment I really believed that Mrs Wilkinson, the lady of the house, was about to have a stroke. After all she was elderly, and she went dark red right to the roots of her hair. She no longer clung to life on her own account but, as she said trembling with agitation, England must survive, must be able to live on in freedom. Surely there was no one in England who did not feel the same, no one who was not ready to fight for that freedom.

We were all very moved by the rescue of the British Expeditionary Force in the first days of June. We heard of the astonishing ways in which people managed to help, how private yachts and boats played their part in bringing home the 300,000 men who had been cut off at Dunkirk. We were told how the men waited their turn, calmly and without panic, standing in the water for many hours at a time. For several days Mrs Wilkinson's only subject of conversation with us was this miraculous rescue.

In the midst of these political excitements we never knew whether, with an invasion threatening, we would have to leave England and find some other place of refuge. On the other hand, however, it was doubtful in the extreme whether such a thing would still be possible. Would we not fall into the hands of the S.S. before we could do anything of this kind? At Hamburg we had already had our names included in the list of immigrants to the United States. But in accordance with the system of quotas we had to take our place in the queue and it was still far from being our turn. The waiting lists of those who had prior claims were endless. At that time Cuba was offering a certain amount of assistance to some by issuing visas to those individuals who were able to stay there for a time until they could enter the United States. Anyone who did go to the States was integrated into the community far more quickly than in England. It was only after Pearl Harbour that the same difficulties arose there too which we were already encountering here as a result of the war. At any rate those who were in America no longer had to cope with anxieties as to whether they should continue their journey any further.

Some weeks later, Willand was declared a protected area and once more I and the children had to move. Even before this we had had some restrictions imposed upon us. We were no longer allowed to have a radio or any photographic apparatus, and we were forbidden to leave the house after dark. Where should we go now?

I now thought of Oxford. I did consider certain other possibilities as well, but Oxford was a goal I had had in mind all along. My husband was still interned, and did not yet know that we had to move again. When I told him of it he was satisfied with all the arrangements except that he was always anxious lest it should prove too much for me.

We arrived in Oxford with our fourteen trunks, alarming enough for the landlady of our new boarding house, Mrs Harrison! But she was a very sensible person who understood my position. Through a Spaniard who was a refugee from Franco and who was also staying at the boarding-house she was politically well informed. She lived in a big house in which she let lodgings to undergraduates. It was situated in the most pleasant part of Oxford and had a pretty garden. I and the children together occupied only a single room. After one week when I came to pay my bill, Mrs Harrison said, 'But dear Mrs Leibholz, I am not charging you anything. You are refugees'. I had the greatest difficulty in convincing her that I really could pay the rent. In spite of everything I could in fact still draw upon the small reserves of money which we had brought with us from Göttingen, and also on a small grant which my husband was receiving from the World Council of Churches.

In the evening we used to sit together in Mrs Harrison's living-room-kitchen and listen to stories told us by the Spaniard or, if the air-raid alarm went and we could hear the rumbling of the planes and, very remotely, the explosions, we used to go down to the basement. Whenever planes flew over the Midlands, which was very often, the alarms used to sound for us in Oxford as well. There were several aerodromes round Oxford but not a single bomb ever fell on the city itself. Still planes often used to fly over Oxford. Below in the basement, together with all the English tenants, we would listen to the magnificent speeches of Churchill. Marianne always listened most attentively, whereas Christiane used to whisper pet names into the ear of her toy lamb. At that time Churchill said:

'We shall not flag or fail. We shall go on to the end, we shall fight in France, we shall fight on the seas and oceans, we shall fight with growing confidence and growing strength in the air, we shall defend our island whatever the cost may be. We shall fight on the beaches, we shall fight on the landing

12. Sabine Leibholz with her daughters Marianne and Christiane in 1933

13. Gerhard and Sabine Leibholz with their daughters in 1952 after their return to Germany

14. Gerhard Leibholz

15. Sabine Leibholz

grounds, we shall fight in the fields and in the streets, we shall fight in the hills. We shall never surrender.' Later he said to the Americans, 'Give us the tools and we will finish the job'.

I was relieved that there was no anti-German feeling to be discerned here, but very soon Mrs Harrison found herself being waylaid in the street by people who believed that we had been giving signals to the enemy by flashing torches. Such outbreaks of hysteria did keep occurring every now and then. And now too, posters appeared with the words, 'Careless talk costs lives'.

On the other hand some English people were also naïve to a degree. One day we received a visit from a very nice Dutch lieutenant belonging to the Free Dutch Navy which had been engaged in the struggle against Hitler ever since the occupation of Holland. His uniform really looked like a German one, and it was embarrassing to me to walk through the streets with our guest. After some time English acquaintances asked us in a perfectly friendly way whether we had had a visit from a German naval officer. It remained a mystery to us how they could ever have imagined such a thing.

By now the restrictions on correspondence had been relaxed, and every day the white glazed envelope of Gert's letter lay on my breakfast table with the words 'Opened by Censor' stamped on it in bold print. It was obligatory to use this paper because it was impervious to all known kinds of invisible ink. Provided the writer avoided saying anything relating to politics or the war—something which was by no means so simple—our letters were passed by the censor without much delay, and they were a consolation to us both. In view of the fact that we have hardly ever been separated from one another during our married lives, and have always done everything together, we are now glad to have these letters from one another. Every day now the internees could receive letters, and so every day I made up a little package with some kind of edibles which it was permitted to send. I always took the children with me when I went shopping. Then both of them could choose something for their father.

We found confirmation of a point which Eugen Rosenstock-Huessy explains in his great work, *The European Revolutions*. 'The attitude of the English is relaxed, almost negligent and yet that of a dedicated fighter. The saying "Man is a fighter of his

F

very nature" is typically English. Probably Goethe would have put it slightly differently, "he is a struggler". "Fighter" and "struggler" mean two different things. The struggler feels the whole burden of his earthly nature and his mortality. The fighter is less weighed down by such a sense of burden. The Englishman is not a struggler in the German sense. When King George V was on his deathbed the newspapers wrote, "He is putting up a great fight against death". Racing provided England with an outlet for her chivalry, a way of fighting which was chivalrous without being militarist. Hatred against the king's army and a passion for a noble way of life are both factors which played their part in the devotion to racing which is characteristic of the class which sets the tone in English life. In all these contests the non-militarist element, the element which distinguishes them from a "struggle" in our sense, consists in their competitive character. Any stating of aims always lays one open to irony. An Englishman is careful not to put forward his opinion without some element of self-ridicule. He fights as a cavalier and his opponent fights too. No emotion, therefore, but a certain toughness. . . .

'The attitude of the "fighter" still prevails throughout England. It means being manly, unforced, quiet, not over-dogmatic, and it finds expression in the well-known saying that the Englishman only begins to fight in earnest when he has his back to the wall.'

It was very unfortunate that by the outbreak of war England had made so few preparations for it. In July 1940, after the disaster of Dunkirk, Victor Gollancz published a book entitled *Guilty Men* which came to be so widely read that it went through nineteen editions in two months. The book included severe criticisms of Chamberlain's cabinet. It accused Chamberlain of having failed to pay due heed to the warnings which could be heard from the hustings in Germany. He had failed to appreciate the significance of a whole series of events: the breaking of the Treaty of Versailles, the introduction of conscription, the murders of Dollfuss and Barthou, the occupation of the Rhineland, the war in Spain, the occupation of Austria and Czechoslovakia, and finally the Munich Agreement. The failure to make good use of the period from September 1939 to May 1940 was also made the subject of biting criticism: for instance the fact that progress was far too slow in the manufacture of arms, that there was now a lack of munitions and a lack of aircraft. Wishful thinking, the comfortable self-complacency, and songs such as 'Hang out your washing on the Siegfried line' were here condemned in the strongest terms.

During the aerial bombardment of England, London and the industrial centres were attacked by the Germans with more than two thousand fighter and hunter planes. We were afraid that these were preparations intended to lead up to the invasion itself. After all England was now alone in her struggle, since Hitler had forced the Continent into subjection.

During the period of the 'blitz', we saw that the London underground stations presented a unique picture: Numberless families with hordes of pale children camped out there on the platforms in the most primitive manner. There they ate, slept, knitted, worked and played. During the rush hour there was so little room that one had to be very careful not to tread on somebody. Many of these families no longer dared to venture up at all, and simply remained below although the air was atrocious. Here beneath the Thames was just that one place where one could be sure of escaping from the German aerial bombardment. There was a fear of epidemics but, thank God, it proved unfounded. The fact that the aerial bombardment was brought to a halt was due to the few hundred outstanding English airmen who succeeded in inflicting a quite decisive blow upon the German Air Force.

The Bishop of Chichester did not forget his German protégés in the internment camps. Pastor Hildebrandt, who had likewise been interned, wrote about his visit as follows:

'When the Bishop appeared he could scarcely reply to our welcome. He was almost speechless and could only stammer and stutter. It was an unforgettable moment. The sight of the refugees in their new captivity was just too much for him— it was not only just the question of a wrong to so many of his personal friends, it was a moral burden on the English people. It was clear to him that something must be done immediately. He listened to what we had to say and then acted. On returning from the Isle of Man he called on the central postal censorship office, inspected the stacked postbags of the past six or eight weeks for which the internees had waited in vain, and suggested quietly but firmly that the letters might be delivered to the people to whom they were addressed. Three days later the camp post office was inundated.

'On the 6th August the Bishop raised the question afresh in the House of Lords of the release of the refugees from these camps. He described the high palisades and passages of barbed wire guarded by soldiers, and the crowds of men, gifted, distinguished, and able to be of service, walking aimlessly about condemned to idleness. He clearly defined the difference between aliens of enemy nationality and refugees from the enemy. He asked, "Do you know, my Lords, that in Camp Douglas alone out of 1,900 internees there are 150 who were in concentration camps in Germany?" '

Dr W. Paton, who visited the refugees interned on the Isle of Man, has left this account of his visit:

'I was greatly impressed by the spirit of these men, and especially of the refugee pastors, who, between ourselves, are far finer stuff than the pastors of the congregations in England. ... What impressed me about Hildebrandt, Oelsner and one or two others was the way in which they were finding opportunities for spiritual work in the camps. I was deeply moved and humbled by these men, who seemed to me to be really magnificent Christians.'

One day I heard that those internees who could produce a visa admitting them to America would be released. Immediately I thought of the last piece of advice Dietrich had given me, namely that in case we felt that we should leave England I should seek help from his American friends, Professor Niebuhr, Professor Coffin and Professor Lehmann. The soundness of this advice was really proved, for I received an invitation for Gert, myself and the children and, moreover, my husband was offered a university lectureship. Just then, however, a vessel transporting children to America was torpedoed and because of this we felt that we could not take the responsibility of the voyage.

Here, too, it was the Bishop of Chichester who gave me help where it was most vitally needed. On the 26th July 1940 I received the following telegram from Gert: 'I hope to be in Oxford at half-past six'. I was overcome with joy. I was so excited that my heart began to beat quite wildly and I was really afraid that I would not live through the afternoon. I could hardly bear to have the children skipping about any longer. Three hours later we drove to the station. In my husband's diary the entry for this day consists of only a single word written in large letters: 'Release'.

15

Our lives as refugees during the war years

I thought my husband was looking well, but it was almost four-teen days before he was once more quite the old Gert we knew. For fourteen whole days he really did nothing except write letters of thanks to those of the English who had intervened on his behalf. Now I had moved him to Oxford, something which I had been striving for all along, because I believed that in Oxford we would find lawyers who would have the same professional interests as Gert and English people with whom we would have most in common. And this step did in fact prove to be justified.

Others, too, had been thinking along the same lines, with the result that many refugee professors' families were already living there. Almost all the heads of these families were now in intern-ment camps. Certain criteria were established for deciding which internees should be granted their release, and the various cate-gories of internees were arranged in a definite order of priority. First came the sick on humanitarian grounds, second those who, on grounds of usefulness, were able to contribute to the British war effort or those who employed Englishmen in their own firms. It was surprising how little the political attitude of the internees was taken into consideration.

Every day my husband and I felt fresh joy at being together again. Of course now our anxieties about obtaining work began anew. No jurist with a knowledge of German law could get very far in England. The situation was simply this: those individuals who had fled from their own countries found themselves for the most part in a country that was strange to them, in the midst of a war, without money, and in many cases without having mastered the language of that country. Certainly England did admit the refugee—decency and tradition demanded no less—but this did not mean that the refugee was loved or incorporated into the community.

One night all the innumerable bells of Oxford started ringing and an icy fear fell upon us for this was the signal that the invasion of England was about to take place. The idea was a terrifying one, but soon we could breathe again. It was a false alarm that had been transmitted. Once the aerial bombardment of England was over these fears subsided.

A further point about Oxford was that one never knew how long one could remain where one was staying at any given time. Oxford was crammed. Many Londoners who sought to escape from the nights of bombing used to make the one-and-a-half hours' journey every evening after work in order to come to Oxford. There was a scarcity of lodgings and everyone preferred to take in British people. Here and there quarters were to be had when a husband had been called up and his wife had gone to live with her parents or parents-in-law. It was this sort of situation that gave us our chance. In 1941 we were able to find a small, simple, terraced house to live in which we were able to have completely to ourselves for some eighteen months. The house belonged to a railway official who had joined the army. The furniture was in unspeakably bad taste but this was no longer of any concern to us. On the ground floor there were two living rooms of which one was made over to Gert as a study, for he has not the gift of burying himself in a book or in his work in the midst of disturbances. While we were here we used to go three times a week to an elderly English teacher who also helped us in translating Gert's articles and letters. We were studying English hard and used to go for our lessons as soon as we could in the mornings once I had finished my housework. Here the children had their freedom. They could invite school friends in to visit them and play in the garden.

In our next lodgings difficulties arose for the children. They consisted of three rooms in a handsome house. They were, it is true, attic rooms and the kitchen was situated on the ground floor. The landlady, who seemed to be hysterical, used to persecute our children. She would only allow us to use the back door.

She was also capable of storming into the room with a news-paper and loading us with reproaches for all the crimes which the Nazi régime had committed. It was evident that she did not understand anything of our position. She herself did nothing whatever, had herself waited upon, spoiled her child, and on one occasion when our nine-year-old daughter used the front door she shrieked at her, 'Out! Out! Go to the back door where you belong!' When the Bishop of Chichester visited us at Oxford I deliberately brought him in by our back door which led through the kitchen. Of course this made no difference whatever to him, but I did it in order to shame our landlady. The moment she saw it she at once said that I should have brought the Bishop through the front door. I replied, 'When our guests come to see us they use the same entrance as we do ourselves.' At this she was greatly embarrassed. This woman was not born in England and to this extent she is not typical of England or of English behaviour. At the same time she was the wife of an Englishman who taught at an Oxford college. All this was an unpleasant experience for our children. It was a great joy to me that a cousin of mine, a warm-hearted and resolute woman who had also married a 'non-Aryan' lawyer now lived in England with her four very pleasant children. When she visited us at our lodgings she remarked, 'Whatever has become of you? You do not raise your voice above a whisper and you give the impression of being completely down-trodden. You must leave this place at once.'

About this time refugees who had first gone to Paris after leaving their own country arrived. For them London represented the second refuge to which they had had to flee, and among them were many who had been persecuted on political grounds. Also refugees who had escaped from Norway now sought asylum here. A number of problems arose. Jews who had become assimilated often did not want to be lumped together with orthodox and Zionist Jews, nor did educated men want to be grouped for all purposes with the uneducated.

At this time Dietrich wrote to us from Zürich in optimistic terms: 'We have to be thankful indeed for everything that has been left in order in this chaotic world of ours. You know that we are with you in our thoughts and prayers every day and we know the same of you.... I am sure the day is not far when we shall meet again with unspeakable joy. God be with you and the children and with all of us.'

Our daughters were now going to school in Oxford as day girls. They had particularly able teachers, and a headmistress who was outstanding. In all the English schools to which our children went the teachers were excellent. They never showed the slightest anti-German attitude. Some, indeed, were quite markedly charming to the children. The same could not be said of our daughters' school-fellows in some of the schools they attended. Some of the younger children particularly tried to torment the refugee children on account of their being German and they were unkind to them. We knew of course that these spiteful children only reflected their parents' attitudes. The parents obviously did not differentiate between German Nazis and Germans who had been persecuted by the Nazis, and did not realize how hard it is for a child in a foreign country to cope with spitefulness at school. After having been uprooted, such a child should above all be made to feel secure again. The first time Christiane, aged eight, was insulted for being German Dietrich was still with us in London and he was exceedingly angry. He said, 'We'll clear this up immediately', took Christiane by the hand and walked into the school with her to confront the abusive child. In Oxford there were fortunately a few enlightened parents who did not mind their children making friends with the children from Germany.

It is true that in earlier times in Germany one on the whole moved in the 'circle' of one's parents' acquaintances. But I still remember that when my mother found that one of my fellow pupils at school was a refugee from the old Baltic provinces she immediately did all she could to induce me to befriend her. I had to invite her home several times, but I did have the feeling that she was far beyond me in terms of experience. The Baltic girl was seventeen, a fully developed young woman, and she always went about in a sailor's blouse which had been given her. I was much in awe of her. She smoked and she always wanted to talk about the Russians and about her family's estate. But I was a silly goose of fourteen and wanted to talk about school affairs, and thus my attempts at friendship with Ricarda were not very successful. However meeting her had given me a glimpse of other horizons. Once I was invited to her home, which was extremely crowded.

I found the smoke, the lack of space, the numerous relatives, and the array of bottles on the table somehow strange and disturbing. This was my first experience of the atmosphere of a refugee home, and later when I lived in Oxford it often came back to me.

At first I found the children's school uniform ugly to a degree. The girls wore tunics and a blouse with the school tie. Over this costume was worn a blazer with the school coat of arms embroidered on it. The whole was crowned with a round hat equipped with a ribbon in the school colours. This outfit was in no way picturesque but it proved to be practical in the extreme. A further point in its favour was that it excluded right from the outset all those social distinctions which might otherwise have been expressed in the children's clothes and likewise all discussion of clothes. The children were not allowed to wear either jewellery or lipstick. The general tone of the school was one of good sense, and the teachers' judgements on the qualities of the children as set forth in their school reports were astonishingly sound.

Inside the school buildings all the children felt cold. The coal fires or gas fires provided just enough heat to warm the teachers' backs. The girls wore mittens, and the only solution was woollens and still more woollens, in fact we found the English woollens excellent. Our elder daughter observed everything about her and absorbed it like a sponge. In character she was very mature for her age, and on one occasion when she was ten years old my mother had said of her, 'One can already talk sensibly with her'. I thought so, too. At fourteen her school reports stated, 'She must beware of letting her interests become too academic'. This amused us, as German teachers would never have discouraged academic interests. Actually she had artistic interests, too, wrote children's stories, and drew original, imaginative illustrations for them.

Both children were good at school. After only six months Christiane actually 'jumped' a year. In addition to her schoolwork Marianne gave private lessons, and at sixteen took her college entrance to Oxford. She had an acute awareness of the problems of the refugees. She put down her thoughts about this in a German poem entitled 'The Refugee':

> And as he stood, a shaken hunted creature,
> Chased from the homeland that he loved so much,

The sky that spread its vastness over him
Told him there are no boundaries.

Place after place he learned to leave behind him,
And learns in time what loneliness can mean,
Senses the transience that shines through all,
Pays heed and is most ready for farewells.

He gathers strength. To him no land is foreign;
His fatherland is all the sky defines.
No more, as formerly, will he come home.
He feels it gratefully. His heart is light.

It was sad that our Blüthner grand piano had had to remain behind in Germany, and that there was no instrument in the house for Christiane to use for her practice. At one time there was a clergyman who allowed her to use the piano in his dining-room at specified times and on another occasion we found a family prepared to allow their piano to be used in return for payment. At one time, too, there was a young pianist living in the boarding house in which we were staying. During this time she gave lessons to Christiane and also allowed her to play on her own piano. Most of the pianos were very bad and there were even some in which the owner's darning materials and sewing had their home, resting at the sides above the wires.

The impression that the English children made upon us was that they were more self-assured and independent than the German ones. In their relations with adults they were more direct and more at ease. When they met grown-ups they neither ran away nor stared at them dumbly. For instance they would politely conduct us into the room, invite us to sit down, and attempt in a quite charming way to keep up a little conversation until Mummy or Daddy arrived.

We learnt that apart from court ceremonial it was not the custom for girls to curtsey, but even the three-year-olds were told, 'Give a nice smile.' To me the English children seem to have marked charm even if sometimes they are a little lacking in respect. They seem to have an innate capacity for self-discipline. One morning a lion escaped from a menagerie. A little girl of eight on her way to school came across it in a suburban road. She went to the nearest house, rang at the door and asked politely, 'May I come in? There is a lion in the street!' We found this a typical example of how any outcry or exhibition of fear is avoided, and politeness is preserved at all costs. I believe that in England calm is preserved even in those situations which in other countries are liable to provoke an outbreak of panic.

Our English acquaintances took the problem of education very seriously. Their ideals might be formulated as follows: the child should not be spoiled and should not become destructive or a spoilsport. There should be good fellowship in all fields where the competitive spirit or even jealousy might arise. Each child must learn to restrain its instinct for physical aggression, yet at the same time give of its energy and skill to the utmost. Therefore games are governed by strict rules. Fairness as a principle is deeply instilled even during childhood—for instance children are taught that they must not destroy other children's playthings. It was generally accepted that the child's natural dispositions if unbridled would lead to anti-social behaviour, and that for this reason they had to be disciplined. Perhaps the worst rebuke that could be given was 'That is unfair', and anyone who took advantage of the self-discipline of another, whether in sport or in everyday life, would incur this reproach. We heard that among the working classes, too, excessive competition or thrusting one's way to the top at the expense of others was regarded as unfair, and that this attitude was so deeply rooted that probably in the last analysis it actually diminished industrial output.

I noticed again and again in England that the mothers are less prepared to think that all their geese are swans, and adopt a more critical attitude towards their children than is usual in Germany. In general, English parents are very slow to say anything openly in praise of their young hopefuls, probably because to do so would not be in the best taste.

I felt great admiration for the way in which the young wives of university dons at Oxford coped with their difficulties during the war. Many of them with their three or four children lived in very impractical houses, sometimes still with open fireplaces, yet they did all the work single-handed and never complained. In peace-time English husbands helped a great deal with the daily work and in the evening they often greatly enjoyed giving the children their baths. The father would push the perambulator with the mother walking beside him. We found that in general if an Englishman cannot provide his wife with a household help he takes over as much of the physical work as possible. For instance, he will carry out the dustbins, undertake repairs, polish floors, make fires, clean shoes and do other such chores. Now, when the men had been called up, a really heavy burden fell upon the shoulders of the young wives here as in all countries. It struck us that the first thing the English soldiers did when they came on leave was to take off their uniform and put on civilian clothes. Only then did they feel themselves at home once more.

We discovered that it was incorrect to open a conversation by asking an Englishman about his work. They disliked the attitude of those for whom work and business are more important than their 'way of life' — that mode of living, acting and conducting himself by which the individual realizes the potentialities of his own human personality to the fullest possible extent. The whole professional side of his life is subordinated to what a man thinks, feels and actively engages himself in apart from his work. A man's achievements are secondary in relation to his status as a 'human being', for his humanity must never be viewed as designed for any one specific purpose. We found that Englishmen of all classes were extremely sensitive on this point.

In 1940 a congregation of refugees was formed in Oxford. Pastor Kramm, who had studied at Mansfield College, had remained in England and he now became our pastor. We were able to hold our German Lutheran service at four o'clock on every second Sunday at St Mary's where at all other times the services that were held were those of the Church of England. Dr Kramm was a kind minister and a true pastor and helper. Marianne embarked eagerly upon her confirmation classes together with one other little girl. In 1943 she was actually confirmed in St Mary's Church. We had always hoped that Dietrich would confer confirmation upon her, but the years passed by and we did not want to delay it any longer. After Pastor Kramm's service there was always a meeting in the old library above the vestry where one had tea and talked to the other members of the congregation. The pastor's sole source of income was, as often in England, the proceeds from our collections. Since he was unmarried he found this adequate. He was a Lutheran, intelligent, and took a strong interest in secular politics as well as those of the Church. Unfortunately he died while still very young soon after the war had ended.

From Boar's Hill, the view over Oxford with its innumerable towers is quite enchanting. But only when one has personally experienced life at Oxford can one savour its beauties calmly and to the full, and only then do these beauties become rooted in one's heart.

In the gardens of St John's, as also in those of other colleges, one found oneself in such an atmosphere of quiet and withdrawal that one fancied oneself back in the world of the Middle Ages. One could read there quite undisturbed while quiet gardeners mowed the lawns or tended the herbaceous borders round the old walls. Here the noisy world in Cornmarket Street, with men and cars streaming out of the Morris works, receded into the background and became inaudible. The fronts of the colleges facing outwards onto the street are of course wonderful, but we found that the supreme beauty of these colleges lies concealed behind their doors.

During the war the idea of travelling or holidays never entered our heads, but from spring to autumn we spent many hours in the various college gardens when the weather allowed it. I have never managed to read so much as in England although I had so much work to do. It was not only a joy but a sheer necessity for we still knew so very little of England. I read English biographies, English history, the great classics of English literature, and many recent publications in the fields of religion and politics by writers with whom we were personally acquainted. In this we found the city and college libraries very helpful and also Blackwells, with its wide range of books. At Blackwells one could leaf through any book and read for hours at a time undisturbed. It was generally quite difficult to find anyone who was willing to sell one a book. Almost every day we used to change our books at the city library. It was Marianne who introduced us to the works of W. H. Auden, T. S. Eliot, C. Day Lewis, Christopher Isherwood, Stephen Spender, Louis MacNeice and many other modern writers.

What their musical evenings meant to the Germans, literary societies meant to the younger generations of the English. They delighted in readings of poetry and plays and they also composed strikingly good poetry even at a relatively early age. We thought that the Oxford undergraduates were astonishingly good actors. I believe that a gift for acting is characteristic of the English in general.

One point caused us amazement. Marianne had been speaking about German poetry and the connection which exists in this between death and love, a connection which is surely undisputed. But a young Englishman who had studied German literature replied, 'Really, I do not see the least connection between love and death. This seems absurd to me. There really is no connection between the two'. The German 'mystique of love and death' clearly puzzled him.

It seemed to us that eccentrics flourished at Oxford. I remember one well-established Oxford don, a good friend of ours, who used to go for a three hour's walk through the country every afternoon and arrived to have tea with us one day dripping wet. I asked him whether he would not like to change his socks and put on my husband's slippers. Before I could show him out of the dining-room he was already in his bare feet and had hung his stockings in front of our open fireplace where they steamed away merrily. But his cuffs, too, were wet and he showed me sadly that they were completely frayed. He remarked that he did not like to pay money for such things; that to him a shirt was worth no more than five shillings, and he was not going to pay any more for it now. We noticed that in contrast to the average German the Englishman loves his old suits, his old raincoat, and feels embarrassed in new clothes. Nor is it fortunately any source of pride to him to have a new car. It is too conspicuous and really all that is required of a car is that it should go. For the majority of Englishmen that is enough. Again in contrast to the average German, Englishmen like old-looking luggage. A leather trunk must be inconspicuous. Often the chests, suitcases and trunks which we saw going on journeys were the strangest collection of objects, and in many cases bound round with cord. We liked that.

We felt that the English find eccentricity fascinating, or that at least they are extremely tolerant in their attitude towards it. If a lady in Germany keeps forty-eight cats and puts her whole house at their disposal, people say that she is mad. But such a lady actually lived in our street. Here in England her neighbours used to remark, 'She really does love cats, doesn't she? They can be such darlings, can't they?' Sometimes I had the impression that the English regard the babel of voices rising up from the human race as one great divinely ordained symphony in which there is a place for each individual to make himself heard. Among the artists, men of letters, and professors we found many cranks; in Germany they would have been called over-wrought neurotics, cantankerous or temperamental individuals.

We were now living in a boarding house again, but no longer with kind Mrs Harrison, whose students had returned. Once when we had gone to London for a few days I noticed on our return that in the interval someone had been sleeping in my bed. I remarked upon this to the landlady, who looked at me with the utmost astonishment and remarked, 'Yes, that was only Jack. He was here for the weekend'. Jack was her son who was in the Air Force. When I asked for clean sheets she was most offended.

Her boarding-house was kept in order by two cleaning women. In this house, formerly a private residence, there were only two baths with two adjoining washbasins. The fifteen guests were free to use these at specified times which had to be adhered to. Fortunately hot water was always available for baths through a gas geyser in which one had to put shillings. It was for each one to leave the bath and washbasin clean behind him. But for me the standard of cleanliness always left something to be desired, and we always went to the bathroom armed with a large bottle of disinfectant in addition to the sponge-bags and towels over our arms.

For us exiles the situations which arose during those years were so strange to us, and the circumstances in which we lived were so different from those we had known, that sometimes I seemed to be living in a fairy tale, and I used to ask myself, 'Is this really me or not?' But again and again a sense of humour came to one's rescue and the difficulties were surmounted.

We noticed that it was taken for granted that the master of the house helped his wife in the domestic routine. He helped in serving breakfast and with carving the meat. However it clearly would have been unthinkable for him to pour the tea. This belonged absolutely and exclusively to the mistress of the house. More-over, whatever guests she had to tea—invited or uninvited—she had to remember who took two lumps of sugar in their tea and who took only one, which guests liked their tea without sugar and which prefered it with or without milk. I was not at all good at remembering this. Even during the time of the 'Battle of Britain' the ritual of serving tea still continued. It struck us that the husband passed the cups round, that no gentleman remained sitting while a lady was on her feet and that he would always rise when she entered the room, repeating this gesture every time she left or returned. In Germany the gentleman only stands up once, when he is introduced.

At Oxford some of the dons used to invite us to tea at their colleges, for they understood that although as Germans we were branded as 'enemy aliens' we did not in the least fit into this category. We learnt that it was correct to take one's leave after three quarters of an hour, often just as one had embarked upon a discussion. But a compensating factor was that in this way the whole afternoon was not taken up by the visit. On one occasion before we were aware of this we went to have tea with one old lady who soon quite evidently began to be alarmed lest we should prolong our stay and she would have to invite us to dinner. Accordingly she brought us to our feet by kindly conducting us into her garden in order to 'look at the flowers' (although there were hardly any to be seen) and then standing at the garden gate so that it became clear to us that we should bring our visit to an end. Once when we arrived for tea five minutes after half-past four we noticed that this had earned us a black mark for discourtesy. There were so many different customs to be learned. For instance, our children had just learned that in Germany one leaves one's left hand lying on the table during meals. Here, on the other hand, they had to keep their hands under the table. Again it astonished us to see people cutting their potatoes with their knives. Another point which I found it difficult to think of in time was that I had to be the first to greet the gentlemen of my acquaintance whom I met in the street. Finally I became accustomed to this, but afterwards when I returned to Göttingen I shocked the gentlemen by retaining this habit. Yet another point to remember was that one had never to enquire the nature of anyone's profession or that of his father, and this caused many a difficulty.

It was a great relief to me that anti-Semitism towards my husband or children no longer constituted any problem whatever here. Anyone who was baptized was a member of the

Church and his 'race' was of no concern. This is not to say that there is no anti-Semitism in England, but we found no trace of it in our case, and all during the persecution of the Jews by Hitler anti-Semitism never found any foothold in England. Such coldness and hostility as we did meet with here arose from the fact that we were Germans.

In September 1953 the *Deutsche Rundschau* published a poem entitled 'Exile' which my daughter Marianne had written previously in English and later translated into German:

> *He's often startled—rain, the sounds and smells*
> *knocking up visions of another age*
> *he shared in—that is over—*
> *a stage surrounds the thwarted looker-on*
>
> *His roots, still bleeding, sore from the uprooting*
> *curl inwards now on striking granite ground.*
> *This circle's closed.*
> *He's outside, near to fainting—*
>
> *Walking the city streets on rainy nights*
> *sensing the lamps and voices toss and swim*
> *grasping a fence to see if it is real*
> *a smell of rain-washed pine-trees startles him—*
>
> *I am a symbol—and he lurches, stumbles—*
> *he sees a solitary star, he stands.*

A little before April 1942 we sent Dietrich some photographs of our children. In return he wrote to us as follows:

'You can hardly imagine what a joy the photos were for me and the rest of the family. Marianne has such an open, good and most intelligent face. There can be no doubt that she will make her way and be a great joy and help to you. Christiane is still the same lovely friendly girl she has always been.... What about Marianne's confirmation? ... I hope Marianne will have a good time with your Methodist minister. It is so important that she finds her way to Christianity and the Church. There are so many experiences and disappointments which lead to nihilism and resignation, especially for sensitive people. So it is good to learn early enough that suffering and God are not a contradiction but rather a unity, for the idea that God himself is suffering is one that has always been one of the most convincing teachings of Christianity. I think God is nearer to suffering than to happiness, and to find God in this way gives peace and rest and a strong and courageous heart. I was moved so much about what you wrote me about the ninetieth psalm and about the verse Marianne likes so much: 'Wait upon the Lord....' How much I would like to talk to her about all that! As my godchild she is particularly in my heart and in my prayers....'

In Berlin they were anxious about our future. As late as March 1941 on a journey to Zürich, Dietrich wrote to one of our acquaintances who had emigrated to Brazil to ask him to help us to continue our journey there:

'My parents (and of course all of us) are very grateful to you for all that you have written to us about Sabine. So far everything is going quite well for us all. Susi has not yet made her journey to the mountains with the children. But it will probably still be necessary. However the times still cause our parents great distress. For elderly people it is really rather too much! My work continues as before. Do you not know of anything good for Gert in Brazil? The last letters sounded rather depressed. It would be such a relief—beyond all comparison. But I am well aware of how difficult this is now. Perhaps, however, something will still turn up....'

At that time the Bishop of Chichester sent us a letter from Visser 't Hooft about Dietrich:

19th March 1941
The Rt Rev. The Lord Bishop of Chichester,
St Martin's Vicarage,
Brighton.

Dear Bishop,
Many thanks for your telegram which has reached Dietrich just before he returned home. It will mean a great deal to him to have this message. He was a week with us and spent most of his time extracting ecumenical information from persons and documents. It is touching to see how hungry people like

him are for news about their brothers in other countries, and it is good to know that he can take back so much which will encourage his friends at home.

On the other hand, we learned a lot from him. The picture which he gave is pretty black in respect to the exterior circumstances for the community which he represents. The pressure is greater than ever. But fortunately he could also tell us of many signs that their fundamental position has not changed at all and that they are as eager as ever for fellowship. Many of them have really the same reaction to all that has happened and is happening as you have or as I have. And this is remarkable after such a long period of isolation. . . .

I greatly admired the elderly among the refugees, how they came to terms with their lot and reconciled themselves to the course of events. They were so pleased to see the younger generation developing and proving themselves at school, as students, or in their professional life. We were a very heterogeneous group of individuals, yet at the same time we were one great community bound together by a common fate. Many young people between twenty and thirty were already helping to support their elderly parents by working as nurses, opticians, housekeepers, or shop assistants. Most of them, it is true, would have gone to the university in Germany and were capable of following other callings.

In Oxford we had to change our lodgings six times. Since we did not possess a single piece of furniture in England, and had neither household linen nor kitchen utensils it was not all that difficult. On the other hand, however, it is unpleasant to live with one's family for nine whole years out of fourteen trunks, several of which contained books and manuscripts, and which, for want of space, could hardly ever be unpacked. I remember in Holland the sorrowful look that my father cast in my direction when he saw me burrowing in the trunks.

In those years in England, however, I actually discovered something about myself, namely that since aesthetically speaking there was so little to give us pleasure in our furnished lodgings I could completely detach myself from my surroundings. I might even say that the situation had an 'interiorizing' effect upon one. One lived in a more spiritual atmosphere than is the case in Germany today.

The losses which the English families had to bear also affected us very deeply. Our English friends were extremely restrained in times of mourning, and they made the greatest efforts to hide their grief. But when we entered the room they would still lovingly show us the photograph of a fallen son or husband, and at such times the face that looked out so kindly from the photo would be there very vividly and make us wince.

One morning in 1940 the children discovered that the word 'Oxford' on the board over the Oxford High School had been painted out with black paint. Everywhere in the city the word 'Oxford' had been obliterated. This had been intended as a precautionary measure against parachute troops so that they would not be able to know where they were. In many places even the large boards on the stations were removed. To us these measures appeared naïve. At the same time, too, obstacles were stretched over the broad expanses of lawn at Oxford and these were intended to prevent landings.

Again and again in my daily life the impression was borne in upon me that it is 'fair play' that lies at the roots of the English way of acting. Most Englishmen have a natural sureness of touch which enable them to bring their own concerns into harmony with the interests of the community as a whole. In connection with the black market, moral standards were very high. I do not even know whether there was any real black market at all. Standing in queues was borne without complaint, although it was very tiring. Rationing was introduced at a very early stage to cover fats, sugar and meat. It was necessary to exercise extreme economy in almost all such commodities. We learnt that the English are great meat eaters who found the smallness of the meat ration hard to bear. Yet no-one actually needed to go hungry in England during the war. There were also a few English people who begrudged the refugees everything. Once when Marianne was fetching our meal from the landlady of the boarding-house her grown-up daughter said, 'Mummy, why do you give these people anything to eat?'

For the Germans the tea ration was far more than they needed, and this was something with which we could make our English friends happy. Coffee was never rationed, but at the time it was hardly drunk in England either. Tea was drunk as 'early morning tea' at seven o'clock, as a breakfast drink at nine o'clock, as 'elevenses' at eleven o'clock, sometimes immediately after lunch and in any case always at tea-time at half-past four. Finally one further cup of tea was sometimes taken as a 'nightcap'. We discovered that the nightcap, however, preferably consisted of a hot milky drink. Like the hot water bottle it was part of going to bed. Without a hot water bottle one's bed would seem cold and clammy after one's bath, for the bedrooms were quite unheated. Every evening I used to fill between four and six hot water bottles, smooth the sheets warm with them, and put them at the end of the beds nearest the feet. In this way one could at least be warm when one fell asleep.

The English coal for the open fireplaces had a wonderful appearance and was slaty in structure. Great fat gleaming lumps, many of which we had first to break up into smaller pieces, used to arrived in sacks and were simply heaped on the open ground next to the back entrance. During the war coal was rationed because there were too few miners. In spite of the constant damp the coal burned splendidly. However one did always find a layer of black dust on all the furniture in the mornings. It was also a difficult business to 'build' a fire as it should be done. One put on special gloves for the purpose and had an array of tools which one hung on a stand near the fireplace. Sitting before the fire one could sometimes experience something like a miniature hibernation. But you always had to do something to a blazing fire. We found that the English generally knitted or read at the fireside, and we, too, did much reading by the fire. It provides a cosy centre for the room, and later when I returned to Germany I at first missed it very much. For how could one form a group in the evening? Should we perhaps sit in front of the central heating? It was very rare for private houses in England to have central heating. But there were also the more practical gas fires and electric fires, either portable or else built into the fireplace.

We found that the British were really an undemanding people. They neither complained nor lamented. They said 'We mustn't complain must we?' Not to complain, to be patient, was characteristic of the English, they expected this kind of self-discipline of themselves. We, too, made it our rule. Gert, in spite of having grown up in very lavish circumstances so far as space was concerned, was always satisfied with everything. At home he always felt very comfortable whatever the conditions. Not all the refugees reacted in this way. One other point struck me about the social habits of the English, something which we in Germany have lost: one is reticent about saying what one knows. One can have views. One can hold that something 'may well be the case'. But one is not too dogmatic about what one knows. One avoids laying down the law. The English found the German term *Standpunkt*, in the sense of an intellectual position from which one would not budge, quite comical. And in the same way they smiled at the attitude of 'having a particular *Weltanschauung*' or having a particular kind of *Kultur* as being somewhat pretentious.

We discovered that most Englishmen wanted to have a house of their own and that most English people seemed to live in small houses. No doubt this is why London sprawls out so terribly far. This style of living seemed prompted primarily by the great desire which the English have to lead their own lives in their own way. The high walls round many gardens bore witness to this. But just as the Englishman strives to guard his own private sphere of existence, so, too, he respects that of his neighbour. To look into a window as one passes by, we learnt, is something that is simply not done.

Sometimes when the river rose the south of Oxford became flooded. It always surprised me that the houses dried out once more. Even the swans appeared, and our garden was transformed into a pond. At the end of the garden stood a shed with windows, ivy-clad and pretty, which was really a workshop. We had carried our numerous trunks down there, for there was no cellar to the house and apart from this there was nowhere else to put them. When the water rose up we had to put on our wellingtons—every child in Oxford seemed to possess these high rubber boots—and steer the trunks across the pond in such a way that they floated up to the house.

I hardly knew a single Englishman who did not like gardening and did not set aside some time for it or at any rate did not cultivate fine roses. One could hear the clipping of garden shears to right and left as they clipped their privet hedges, and they liked to give us presents of blooms from the plants which had flourished under their hands. They liked also to give advice about gardening. To 'potter' quietly about by themselves with their pipes in their mouths—that was what they enjoyed. We noticed that the man who has a garden often also has a shed, a shelter with a workshop. There he keeps his tools and there, too, he spends much of his leisure time at his numerous hobbies, such as amateur carpentry, the cultivation of plants, repairs, and similar activities. And here his wife does not disturb him. It seemed to be the special task of the father to keep the garden in order. In England we could work in the garden almost the whole year round. Even if it snowed, something which was almost a national catastrophe, still the snow hardly lay for more than a few days. The English seemed never prepared for a fall of snow, which was strange. Frozen water pipes were borne with a smile, even when one had to ask good friends or trusted neighbours to allow one to use their lavatory.

On 22nd June 1941 the news reached England of Hitler's attack on the Soviet Union. Straightaway one sensed a general feeling of relief. 'Now it cannot last all that much longer.' 'Even Napoleon did not manage it.' These and similar opinions were heard.

Hitler's attack was also welcomed because it relieved England from the immediate pressure of the threatened invasion. It was currently held that 'now Hitler has taken on too much and has himself brought about the turning-point of the war'. Maps of Russia were hung up and the positions of the opposing forces marked in. But then the English people were made uneasy after all at the advance of the German troops. White Russia and the Ukraine were overrun. As the advance now proceeded in giant strides an appeal appeared again and again on London walls to 'Open the second front now'. The attacks were brought to a halt before Leningrad and Moscow, for the German army was no match for the Russian winter. In February 1943 the defeated German armies capitulated at Stalingrad and in May 1943 the German and Italian armies surrendered at Tunis. In July 1943 the English landed in Sicily.

In June 1942 we travelled to Cambridge to attend a conference on the 'Christian Fellowship in War-time' at which William Paton was the principal speaker and Gert was also reading a paper. Suddenly the Bishop of Chichester appeared with some typed sheets in his hand and said he wanted to speak to Gert and me. He had come straight from Stockholm and had just had an unexpected meeting with Dietrich there*. He had brought with him

---

* Dietrich had obtained a courier's pass from the defence ministry and it was this that enabled him to make these journeys abroad.

documents from Dietrich relating to the resistance groups and
giving the names of the officers who would collaborate in the overthrow of Hitler, and he gave all of these to us to read. As we read
we felt our hearts pounding. In Switzerland Dietrich had learnt
that the Bishop would be in Stockholm and had straightaway
travelled to Sweden. There he had requested the Bishop to inform
the British Foreign Secretary, Anthony Eden, of all this, to discuss
it with him and as soon as possible to let him know the results of
the discussion. We were shaken. The feeling of having such
recent news of Dietrich combined with the pain of not having
seen him and of knowing that he was back in Germany once more
was terribly agitating. Everything that had taken place at the
Conference vanished from my mind. It was a heavy burden to
us to know of the great danger to which my brothers and sisters,
our friends and these officers were exposing themselves. We were
pleased, it is true, to see how eager and ready the Bishop was to
make contact with Eden as soon as possible. But we were in-
expressibly weighed down by our anxieties as to how all this
would end. And for me there was a further fear. There was a
possibility that someone might not be discreet enough in using
Dietrich's name, and that some mention of it might leak out to the
Press. But in fact nothing of the kind took place. The Bishop had
done his utmost to dissuade Dietrich from returning to Germany
and had sought to take him straight to England with him. But
Dietrich was quite resolute in refusing this in view of all those
who were in contact with him in Germany. He did not want to
be the means of bringing disaster upon anyone. The Bishop was
very sad as he told us this.

Soon further news arrived in which Dietrich told us of the
general deprivation of German nationality which was being inflicted on 'non-Aryans' abroad, and of which we, too, had already
heard. In his letter Dietrich wrote:

As far as I can foresee the future of your fatherland this law
is a good thing for you all, and will only make your return
easier on that day for which we are all longing.

During his stay at Stockhom Dietrich had written to us, amongst
other things:

'I had a most enjoyable time with George*. You will certainly

* George Bell, the Bishop of Chichester.

have had a letter from him, too. I am still optimistic enough to believe that it will not be long till we meet again. My heart is full of thanks for these last days. George is one of the very finest men that I have met in my life.'

Eden's answer was total rejection. His motive for this rejection was clear to us. By now the war had been steered in a nationalistic direction and now it must be fought to the close as part of a nationalistic policy. Again it was probable that one was anxious not to create a breach with the Russians by coming to a separate agreement. Nothing was expected from the German resistance any more. It was forgotten that the compromise policy followed by the English at Munich had prevented a *coup d'état* at that time.

In expressing his disappointment in his reply to Mr Eden the Bishop quoted the words Churchill had uttered in the House of Commons on the 13th May 1940:

"It is our policy to wage war against a monstrous tyranny never surpassed in the dark lamentable catalogue of human crime." 'If there are men in Germany' [wrote the Bishop] 'also ready to wage war against the monstrous tyranny of the Nazis from within, is it right to discourage or ignore them? If we by our silence allow them to believe that there is no hope for any Germany, whether Hitlerite or anti-Hitlerite, that is what in effect we are doing.'

On the 13th July the Bishop had an interview with Sir Stafford Cripps. He also approached Mr Winant, the United States Ambassador of the time, with the same request.

Up to the autumn of 1943 we had still been able to obtain fragmentary scraps of news about our parents, brothers and sisters and friends through the World Council of Churches at Geneva. This was a great consolation to us. A friend of Dietrich's, Dr E. Sutz, a Swiss minister from Zürich, kindly acted as a go-between to bring news from one section of our family to the other. On the last birthday he spent in freedom Dietrich was sitting by the sick-bed of our sister Christel, who had undergone an operation. She wrote as follows: 'He came to see me with a bottle of champagne and a delightful little almond tree, and to-gether we drank to other times.'

As soon as I heard of the arrest of my brother Dietrich, together with my brother-in-law, Hans von Dohnanyi, and my sister Christel on the 5th April 1943 I broke off all contact by letter. My reason for doing this was my great anxiety lest I might in some way bring still greater trouble upon the prisoners by sending them news and so revealing that they had been in contact with us. It was a terrible anxiety to carry around with one. From the late summer of 1943 onwards we were completely cut off. While I was preparing breakfast for the children and my husband at a quarter to eight I used to turn the radio on. First a few brief minutes of morning prayers were broadcast, and immediately following this the news was read. Almost every day one heard, 'Our bombers were out over Germany last night with Berlin as their target. Three of our aircraft have not returned.' Or else it was reported, 'Our bombers were again over the Ruhr area'. In the children's school a poster was hung up with the words, 'Ten shillings for a bomb on Berlin'. Thus every morning began with anxious thoughts which were focused chiefly upon relatives and friends, most of whom lived in Berlin.

Taken as a whole our time in England represented an epoch in our lives which none of us would wish to have missed. We were thrown into contact with people from the most varied walks of life, and our horizon was immensely enlarged. We collected experiences which we would never have been able to have had we merely been travellers. In those years we spent in England we got to know not only the English themselves but citizens from the British Commonwealth as well, Canadians, Indians, New Zealanders, Australians and South Africans, all with their own national characteristics and ways of life, of which up till then we had known nothing. It was natural that England should have had a much stronger orientation towards the Commonwealth than towards the Continent. A child at school might not know where Czechoslovakia was, but it would be familiar with the geography of all the Dominion countries. At Oxford the upper strata among the students took a special interest in their fellow students from India and Africa. These students who came from the Dominions did in fact constitute the élite of their own countries.

We met university teachers from India, Canada and South Africa, and had interesting conversations with them. We also talked with Australian farmers and persuaded them to tell us about life in their country. We were interested not only in the facts they told us but also in the outlook they themselves represented and in the way of life which they followed.

During all these stimulating encounters with so many individuals who were strange to us and the tension of all the political developments, the petty toils of everyday life continued. As a housewife, I soon overcame a certain prejudice against New Zealand butter and New Zealand eggs, for they were in fact excellent products and much cheaper than fresh English eggs or English butter. We also ate Australian rabbit meat. It could not be accounted a delicate dish but it could be obtained off the ration because it was imported in great quantities. South African wines and South African tinned fruit and fresh fruit, too, were good. How it was possible for even Chinese eggs to taste fresh I could not understand. In the children's diet, peanut butter played a major part; fat being very scarce the children devoured this off-ration product by the spoonful.

Gradually we learned to celebrate our Christmases with English carols and English dishes, Christmas pudding and mince pies. Among my most beautiful memories of England are the carol services in the college chapels. Some of the choir boys had angelic voices, and they sounded like something from another world. The magic of the Christmas carols is unique. No *Thomaner-Chor*, no *Domspatzen* choir can ever be a substitute for the Oxford choirboys singing their Christmas carols. These services became our real Christmas. Of course we always sang our German carols, too, with the children, but even to me, to whom the German carols meant so much from childhood, the English carols were just as dear. In the old days I would never have believed that such a thing could be possible.

During this period Gert was also actively engaged in political matters. At that time the more far-sighted among the English were beginning to concern themselves with the aims to be striven for when peace was declared. It is true that these questions were completely thrust aside by the Vansittartists, the adherents of Lord Vansittart, the implacable opponent of the Germans. I remember a conference with William Paton, who was General Secretary to the World Council of Churches. He was considered the prototype of a Christian politician yet he visualized the future completely from the point of view of power politics. He considered at the time that Russia and the Western Powers were pursuing the same goals in central Europe. I can still hear him at the conference defending the opinion that by the end of the war the Russians would be so weakened that they would be dependent upon the English. Even then this seemed to us totally mistaken. Although William Paton had access to the Foreign Office, and was considered to be the great Christian politician, he was actually capable of making such statements! At this time Stalin had said, 'It is a calumny against the Red Army to maintain that it is its goal to destroy the German people or to annihilate the Germans as a nation. The Red Army neither has, nor can have, any such idiotic aims. It would be ludicrous to identify Hitler's clique with Germany as a state or with the German people. The experience of history shows that Hitlers come and go while the German people and the German nation remain.'

In a lecture delivered at the time, Gert stated that after the war Germany would still always be in a position to choose between East and West, and that for this reason the Western Powers should shape their political aims so that Germany would prefer to align herself with the West. They should do this by putting forward from the Western point of view proposals corresponding to those which Stalin was putting forward from his.

The Bishop of Chichester had long been bringing pressure to bear to ensure that now at last, before the Western offensive began, the necessary distinctions should be recognized and the difference between the Hitler régime on the one hand and Germany on the other should be formally expressed. The Lord Chancellor, Lord Simon, actually did this in the following statement:

'I now say in plain terms on behalf of his Majesty's government that we agree with Premier Stalin first that the Hitlerite state should be destroyed, and secondly that the whole German people is not (as Dr Goebbels has been trying to persuade them) thereby doomed to destruction.'

At the time the B.B.C. reported this statement of policy in its broadcasts to Germany.

A further matter which the Bishop of Chichester found weighing most heavily upon his conscience was the question of the indiscriminate and 'blanket' bombing of non-military and non-industrial targets by which such terrible losses were inflicted upon the civil population in Germany. When it was indicated to him from authoritative quarters that he should not speak about this he wrote about it in ecclesiastical journals, and here, too, he found an agreement which was denied to him elsewhere in official circles. He stated at that time:

'When a minister of the government speaks in exulting terms of a ruthless and destructive bombing of the German people; or quarters supposed to be authorative contemplate the subjection of fifty German cities to the same terror as Hamburg (or Coventry) has suffered, or the wiping out of Germany as an industrial unit. then we have a real cause to grieve for a lowering of moral tone, and also to fear greatly for the future.... To bomb cities as cities, deliberately to attack civilians quite irrespective of whether or not they are actively contributing to the war effort, is a wrong deed whether done by the Nazis or by ourselves.'

The Bishop sought to work against the feelings of revenge which arose as a result of the sufferings, the losses and the prolongation of the war. He sought to prevent men from throwing overboard now the ideals for which England entered the war. From 1943 onwards the attacks upon Germany had become ever more terrible. And accordingly in February 1944 he laid his accusations before the House of Lords. For the government, Lord Cranborne spoke in defence of the Royal Air Force. At that time we used regularly to read the *Spectator* and the *New Statesman*, and were very glad that in these journals at any rate there was agreement with the Bishop, whereas elsewhere many voices in the Press were raised against him. Liddell Hart, the military correspondent, did believe, it is true, that a very large proportion of the silent public stood behind the Bishop, and we personally met many English people, especially among the young, who actually spoke out energetically against the indiscriminate bombing of the German cities.

The Bishop was not only a man of prayer; he was a statesman as well. It is only in retrospect that he has come to be better understood. He followed his conscience. There can be no doubt that he would have had a considerable chance of becoming Archbishop of Canterbury, and that it was his speeches during the war that lost him this chance. This is something of which he was perfectly well aware. But opportunism was foreign to his nature. He knew that Churchill would never favour his promotion or act to secure his advancement in the Church.

During the war there were fewer students at Oxford, and the chances for exiled German professors to find any work were, therefore, even less than in peace-time. An exception to this occurred in 1942, when my husband was asked to give some lectures at Christ Church by Professor L. Hodgson. Professor Hodgson had heard Gert speaking at the Conference of the 'Christian Fellowship in War-time', and soon afterwards he asked him to give these lectures. Lord Lindsay, the Master of Balliol also invited Gert to lecture on 'The Nature of Democracy'. During these years Gert interested himself chiefly in Political Science, although it was only after the war that he actually taught in this field. In general it could be said that during the war years those exiled German scholars who were specifically jurists could not find teaching posts in the university. Most of them eked out their existence by means of stipends which they drew, for instance, from the Society for the Protection of Science and Learning, which had been brought into being by the English on humanitarian grounds. Even so the help they could give was only sufficient to enable these scholars and their families to live in circumstances of great poverty.

The women refugees too, many of whom came of good families, lived for the most part in depressing circumstances. Frequently they had to take posts as domestic servants in English families and their experiences there were often hurtful and humiliating. Even though they were highly praised for the excellence of their work, and were soon quite indispensable, they were still not accorded the consideration which was their due. Occasionally they were actually given different names, for instance the name of the last cook employed at the house concerned. In other words their employers did not so much as take the trouble to accustom themselves to the new names! It was not malice on the part of the English employers, but a total failure to imagine what the position of a refugee must be like. They showed themselves incapable of understanding what it meant for someone whose social background was actually similiar to theirs to be forced, for lack of resources, to accept work as a housemaid. For us it was depressing to be forced to look on this struggle for existence without being able to help. Sometimes it seemed to me a strange instance of the will to stay alive in the midst of the storm.

One day we received an unexpected visit from Dr Berkenau,

a psychiatrist who had formerly been a senior doctor under my father at the University Hospital of Berlin. Subsequently he had had to flee from the country and had found a post at the Warneford in Oxford. He now arrived with the *Lancet* in his hand and showed us an announcement of my father's death together with an obituary notice by one of his former colleagues. After the first shock, however, certain doubts began to arise in our minds as to the correctness of this report, and, thank God, we soon found it was contradicted by other sources of information.

Every year the English way of life became more interesting to us. At this time the ideal of 'gentlemanliness' still seemed firmly rooted throughout all classes in English society. We had a handyman who used to repair anything that got broken in the house, and I will never forget the care and sensitivity with which he treated his wife. She was expecting her fourth child. There was so little money that when they were in their house and yard the family used to wrap their feet in rags to save their shoes. But as soon as the sun shone in the little yard the husband used to sweep it out, then bring out a folding deck chair, help his wife into it, bring her a pillow and blankets, wrap her up in them, and then run his hand lightly and lovingly over her hair. Sometimes he appeared with the teapot in his hand and helped her to a cup of tea.

For a considerable time we lived in a working-class district. The people there were all pleasant and friendly to us, and we even had the feeling that they were glad that we had come to live among them. No aversion to foreigners prevailed here such as we encountered from many sides among the upper middle classes at Oxford. The working-class people were more human. They were interested in how we got on as aliens in their country. 'Do you keep your family simply by what you have in here?' asked one man of my husband, tapping his forehead as he did so. And when my husband nodded he said, 'You must have a wonderful brain'.

We particularly enjoyed visiting Christopher Dawson, a very distinguished writer on the philosophy of cultures, and his wife. He was then in his early fifties and lived above Oxford at Boar's Hill in a beautiful house with a splendid garden. Previously Christopher had taught philosophy of religion and history of culture at Exeter, and he was now the editor of the famous

Catholic journal, *The Dublin Review*. But later he had to give up the editorship because his views were too liberal. As a Christian humanitarian he was not merely an Englishman but a European, too. He was extraordinarily interested in all that was going on in Europe, which was something quite unusual. The majority of the English at that time had little understanding of Europe. Moreover he fully understood what our state of homelessness meant to us.

Almost every fortnight we went to Boar's Hill and Christopher used these opportunities to discuss political, legal and historical questions with Gert. The stifling of the spirit in the secular modern mass democracies depressed him intensely. It was during this period that he wrote his book, *The Judgement of the Nations*.

In 1944 we once more had to change our quarters, and the only place which we could find to rent was a large furnished house. I sublet one room to an officer of the Free Polish Fighting Forces. The old house was situated by the canal and was plagued with mice. We were lucky not to have rats as well! We waged a hopeless war against the mice. I had to shut everything edible in biscuit tins. In the morning my first task was to empty the traps, something which I found extremely disagreeable but which would have been still more nauseating to Gert. Probably we should have kept three cats, but I cannot stand cats. In the end I found a charwoman who used to come in the mornings and performed the task with a smile—and also with a cigarette in her mouth! She smoked and smoked almost the entire morning through until she had finished her work—smoking made her feel carefree.

Once when we had no help and were all sick in bed our neighbour very kindly brought us a jug of soup, stood it before the door, rang the bell, and vanished. Next day Gert's temperature was normal, but he would not allow me to get up because in my case the doctor thought there was some risk of pneumonia. The children were still in bed with temperatures. 'I'll do the cooking, then,' said Gert, never having done any such thing in his life. I feared the worst. I asked him to bring me the carrots and potatoes so that I could prepare them in bed, and suggested that he should just cut us a little cold meat and bring up the dishes. I told him exactly how long the vegetables would have to be cooked. 'Yes, that's easy,' he replied. He would go downstairs to his study, look at the clock, and then bring up the food when it was cooked. Twenty minutes later I smelt burning and then heard

G

Gert running upstairs. There he stood before me with two black saucepans in his hands, quite upset and sorrowful as he held out the burnt food to me. He had not put in any water!

It is usual to credit the English not only with sound common sense but with a gift for ingenious and constructive compromise as well. In every conversation with undergraduates or dons one felt their readiness for this. They would ask quite indignantly, 'Are you helping to reach a solution or merely contributing to the problem?'

This latter approach was not welcomed.

Any failure to listen to the points of view of others, or any tendency to monopolise the discussion, was considered intolerably bad form. We began to have a very good understanding of the undergraduates who came to the house for tutorials with my husband. They were sent to Gert by various colleges armed with a personal report from one of the college tutors. We were very amused by the way in which one was introduced, simply as 'Stupid but tries hard'. This we found disarming. We discovered that in England the factor of character is never underestimated. We received the impression that many of the English are late developers. The seriousness of mature manhood comes relatively late.

On the whole the undergraduates were a friendly, open group who took an active interest in things. They used to come to tea with us too, and wanted to know all kinds of things about Germany. They showed no prejudice against foreigners. For the most part they were intelligent and well-informed and knew what our position was. We never found any Vansittartists among them. It is true that by then the war was for all practical purposes already won. Several of them were very critical of various measures taken by their own government. In talking to Gert they certainly never stood upon ceremony but they were never over-familiar either.

The generations were then closer to each other in England than in Germany. Sports such as fishing, golf, riding and hunting which the older generation engaged in helped to constitute a bond between them and the young. It struck us that both men and women in England continued to be spoken of as 'middle-aged' right until they were practically in their eighties. Only then were they spoken of as being 'old'. The older generation took a lively interest in the young, and had a strong feeling of responsibility towards them. The young would also confidently turn to some friend of their father's when they needed to ask questions or seek advice or wanted to obtain some help in their careers.

It is a fact that the average English university teacher found it in many cases impossible to undertake any work in collaboration with his German counterpart. Probably this was connected with the calmly pragmatic approach of these English dons to their intellectual work and to their way of conceiving of things altogether as a concrete whole. The fact remains, however, that they did entrust their students to these German professors.

We once met an eighty-year-old theologian who lived in a fine house at Oxford. He described to me how he used to sit at the feet of my great-grandfather, Karl von Hase, the Church historian at Jena. And he told me that Hase was the only real gentleman whom he met in Germany. On another occasion he pulled a photograph of my great-grandfather out of his coat pocket and gave it to me together with an 1835 edition of his *Life of Jesus*. This great-grandfather of mine was born in 1800. At the age of thirty he visited Goethe and describes this visit in his *Annals of my Life*. He was again received by Goethe on the occasion of his appointment as professor at Jena. In 1820, while still a member of the student corporation, he had been imprisoned in the Hohenasperg fortress by the King of Württemberg and later he wrote a history of the Church and other theological books. At the beginning of his history of the Church he wrote:

'Everything has its time. The Lord of time is God. The turning-point in time is Christ. The right spirit of the times is the Holy Spirit.'

When he died students carried his coffin in a torchlight procession for a lying-in-state in the principal church of the city. The flag of mourning was flown over the city hall in memory of this honorary citizen of the city of Jena. To this very day his statue stands in front of the university at Jena, and is also respected by the East German authorities.

16

The invasion and the end of the war

At last the end of the war seemed to be in sight. On the morning of the 6th June 1944 we were just leaving the house when our neighbours' son, who was sitting on the garden fence, called out to us, 'Today is D Day!' We did not quite understand what he meant, but supposed he was trying to say that he had a holiday from school. So we merely replied 'Yes, dear' and continued on our way. Some minutes later Marianne arrived breathlessly on her bicycle telling us the news that English and American troops had landed in France. Great excitement reigned throughout the city. No one spoke of anything else. No one could wait for the newspapers. The tension was enormous. Two divisions had landed by air and about five divisions by sea with the Navy and Air Force in support. Battleships, cruisers and destroyers were sent in and great quantities of materials and vehicles for war were landed in Normandy.

On 13th June the first V.1 weapon landed in England. Many women confessed to me that they were very anxious, but none of them had any doubt of the approaching defeat of Germany. The V.2 was seldom discussed. During these weeks up to the end of August, when de Gaulle entered Paris once more, we devoured all the news from morning to night. At this time, too, the first Canadian regiments arrived in Oxford. We saw how blooming and abounding in strength these fine looking young men were, in contrast to us pale island dwellers. I thought to myself, 'These soldiers cannot fail to advance and conquer, carrying all before them'.

In July 1944 the English troops under Eisenhower broke through the German lines at Arranches. At this stage hopes for peace solidified into plans for peace. Young and old alike were overjoyed at the prospect of being able to visit France and Paris once more. After the landings of the British and American troops in the South, France was soon reconquered. The Nazis had set up concentration camps in southern France and from these the German refugees in England were able to rescue those of their relatives who had survived and bring them back to England. The English authorities were understanding and helpful in this.

On the 20th July 1944—Gert had just returned from a conference of theologians at Hawarden—Marianne burst into the room with the news that an attempt had been made on Hitler's life. My husband asked immediately, 'Revolution or revolt?' Marianne did not know. We hurried to the wireless. We were indescribably excited for it had been a long time since we received our last letters from our brothers, brothers-in-law or friends, and we no longer knew what the opposition were doing over there. What was happening?

On the 20th July 1944 Colonel Klaus Graf Schenk von Stauffenberg brought a bomb into the headquarters of the Fuehrer. Stauffenberg *could not shoot because he had only one eye and two fingers and these only on his left hand*. The bomb exploded but Hitler was only slightly injured. Stauffenberg, who had watched the explosion from a certain distance, immediately flew to Berlin convinced that the attempt had been successful. The Resistance movement in Germany itself and in the occupied territories proceeded to take action as they had planned. The Military Commandant of Berlin, my uncle General Paul von Hase, mobilized the troops under his command and also had the quarter where the government offices were surrounded. Then suddenly Hitler himself spoke to the people over the radio, and immediately the Nazis hastened to take counter-action. With the assistance of Goebbels, who had not yet been apprehended, and of an officer (Remer) who had been given the fullest powers by Hitler over the telephone to put down the revolt, the military strength of the Resistance was broken. The aftermath of the miscarriage of this attempt was that thousands were thrown into prison and four thousand nine hundred and eighty people were executed. The so-called 'People's Court' presided over by Freisler condemned the Resistance fighters to death by hanging or having their heads cut off.

Nowhere in the English Press was any appreciation to be found of the events of the 20th July. Hitler's statement that the attempt was the work of a clique of officers who were ambitious to seize power was accepted. Both the *Manchester Guardian* and *The Times* refused to print articles on the subject.

All along we had made every effort to point out how untrue it was to suggest that any opposition to the evils of the Nazi régime was inspired primarily by the fact that those concerned saw little prospect of a successful outcome to the war or felt that defeat was imminent. On the contrary, this opposition had already been in existence from the moment Hitler seized power. And this despite the fact that Hitler did achieve certain initial successes in the fields of political economy and fiscal policy. It required really endless patience to explain to the English again and again the difference between the Nazi régime together with its adherents and the other Germany which had nothing in common with this.

It was not until October 1944 that the *New English Weekly* decided to publish an article by Gert which represented a different version of the attempt on Hitler's life of the 20th July. In this article, my husband argued, against earlier interpretations, that the significance of the attempt of the 20th July had been unduly played down, and that the motives underlying it had been falsified. He wrote that what was in question here was a movement grandly conceived and inspired by the same humanitarian motives as were upheld in the West. He also stated that the failure of the attempt was a tragedy for the Allies too.

In July 1945 my husband wrote in the *Strand Magazine*:

'Tens of thousands have gone through the fires of persecution, paying with their lives.

For instance most of the leaders of the conspiracy of last July were upholders of the European tradition. And the stand of the Catholic and Confessional Church has filled many people with a new religious vitality.

I fear that plans to put the German educational machinery under the permanent guardianship of an Allied Educational Board are bound to fail because they tend to degrade the trustworthy Germans into quislings in the eyes of the German people. But without putting trust in these elements who are convinced that Germany must again become a European and Christian country Germany cannot be re-educated.

True, the Allies must use political wisdom to get the right people in the right place. But when you do get them, trust them, and let them work under German authority (limiting controls to the political sphere) in order to avert that national humiliation and despair which after the last war so greatly contributed to the present conflict.'

Lord Vansittart, however, was always of the opinion that Nazism could only have grown up in Germany, and that, too, as a consequence of German nationalism and militarism. He rejected every attempt to distinguish between Germans and Nazis. In reply to Gert's arguments, he produced the following angry comments:

'No wise man will agree with Dr Leibholz that the conspirators of last July "were upholders of the European tradition." They were militarists who tardily saw that Hitler had made a mess of their profession. His sin in their eyes was not that he had made war, but that he was losing it. Dr Leibholz deprecates putting German educational machinery under "permanent" Allied guardianship. We don't say permanent but "prolonged". He urges us to have trust in the good Germans. After what has twice happened he cannot expect the victims to have any trust without verification. Germany has forfeited any other kind of trust.

Finally it is utterly false to say that "national humiliation and despair so greatly contributed to the present conflict". This is the old, old propagandist story. Germany enjoyed the greatest prosperity in her history between 1924 and 1929; and the Treaty of Versailles had vanished long before this war. Dr Leibholz must stop trying to sell us this stuff. We have had enough of it.'

Thank God, there were other voices, too, and not merely among the Quakers. It is true that in England it was not understood immediately how much more the German opposition were taking upon themselves when they sought to overthrow Hitler both before and during the war than did the opposition of the Dutch, the Danes or the Norwegians in the German-occupied territories. For these were fighting at the same time against a foreign invader and had their fellow countrymen behind them. The German opposition did not have this support.

Later Lord Vansittart revised his opinions about the Germans.

On the 1st May 1945 news came through that Hitler had committed suicide and so avoided having to answer for his crimes. Already in the last few weeks he had almost become a ghost as far as we were concerned.

On Monday the 7th May we entertained Christopher Dawson and his wife to tea. We had a long discussion about the aims and tasks of peacetime. At that time we did not yet know the pains that would have to be endured or the darkness that still lay ahead for us. On the 8th and 9th May 'Victory in Europe Day' was celebrated. So far as the young were concerned this took the form of noisy celebrations with romping and dancing in the streets. This was how this day was celebrated by the undergraduates at Oxford and the crowds in Trafalgar Square, where a great firework display was mounted. At Oxford St Mary's was full throughout the entire day. The sound of the bells was wonderful. All the churches in Oxford held thanksgiving services, and the undergraduates took part in services in their college chapels.

In London all the churches were thronged to a quite extraordinary extent, so that all day long services were taking place at St Paul's Cathedral and Westminster Abbey. Hour after hour the people who had waited without impatience in long queues before the church doors streamed in. The members of the House of Lords attended service in the Abbey, while those of the House of Commons went to St Margaret's. Their voices must almost have lifted the roof as they sang the hymn, 'O God our help in ages past'. At Canterbury Cathedral five thousand people stood shoulder to shoulder. At Exeter the thanksgiving services had to be prolonged until midnight. The cathedral was floodlit and many had to remain outside sitting on the grass but joining in the singing and the prayers. The great factories in the North released their workers in order to let them attend their churches.

At Westminster Abbey, in the presence of the House of Lords and the Archbishop of Canterbury, a prayer was also read containing the famous words from President Lincoln's historical address of 1865 :

'Grant us, gracious God, that we may strive to bring to completion that task which thou hast given us to perform with malice towards none; with charity for all; with firmness in the right as God gives us to see the right; to bind the wounds of the nations, to care for those who have suffered in the struggle, for the widows and the orphans, and to do all to achieve a just and lasting peace among us and between all nations, through Jesus Christ our Lord. Amen.'

For all of us this was the moment of liberation from the scourge of National Socialism and it brought tears of joy to our eyes.

Soon the war with Japan, too, drew to its close, and we heard then that the Emperor of Japan had asked the Allies to spare his people but had put himself at their disposal. What a different attitude from that of the German leader who took steps to make sure that he would not be called to account in any way for his actions!

17

The post-war years and the return to Germany

Now the war was over. Three long weeks passed, and still no news had come from Germany. On the morning of 31st May, Pastor Rieger telephoned to us from London and asked whether we were at home because he had something to say to us. Gert's reply on the telephone was 'We would be very glad to see you'.

Soon from the window I saw our friend arriving at the house. The moment I opened the door to him I felt fear. The expression of his face was so pale and drawn that I knew that something serious had happened. We quickly entered the room where Gert was, and then Pastor Rieger said with deep sadness, 'It's Dietrich. He is no more—and Klaus too. . .'.

'Oh no, no!' groaned Gert from the very depths of his spirit.

Rieger laid the telegram before us on the table. Then he pulled his New Testament out of his coat pocket and began to read from Mt 10. To this day I still do not know how I lived through those moments except by clinging to every word: '. . . and whosoever shall not receive you, nor hear your words, when ye depart out of that house, shake off the dust of your feet. Verily I say unto you it shall be more tolerable for the land of Sodom and Gomorrah in the day of judgement than for that city. Behold I send you forth as sheep in the midst of wolves. . . . But beware of men: for they will deliver you up to the councils and will scourge you. . . . But when they deliver you up, take no thought how or what ye shall speak, for it shall be given you in that same hour what ye shall speak. For it is not ye that speak, but the Spirit of your Father which speaketh in you. . . . There is nothing covered that shall not be revealed; and hid that shall not be known. . . .

'Whosoever, therefore, shall confess me before men, him will I confess also before my Father which is in heaven. But whosoever shall deny me before men, him will I also deny before my Father which is in heaven. . . . And he that taketh not his cross and followeth after me is not worthy of me. He that findeth his life shall lose it: and he that loseth his life for my sake shall find it.'

Pastor Rieger also read us all the other verses of the tenth chapter, and reminded us of the fact that Dietrich had given so particularly beautiful an exposition of them in *The Cost of Discipleship*.

Apart from this, I no longer know what happened during the rest of this day, but I have not forgotten Gert's face streaming with tears or the sobbing of the children. In the days that followed the worst part of all was waking up in the morning when the whole tragedy would break over one afresh. Work and still more work—that was what helped in these cruel spring months in which the sun and blue sky seemed too much—indeed seemed almost unbearable to one, and even the constant streams of one's fellow men as they passed one in the street seemed only to bring back the question to one's mind again and again: Why should it be precisely you who are still here while those whom we loved so much are no longer with us?

Somehow I had been living wholly for the moment when I could be re-united with Dietrich in a new and better Germany; the moment when we would tell each other our adventures and exchange our news about all that had taken place in these difficult years. Dietrich himself had likewise said in his letters how much he was looking forward to this moment when we would be re-united. Now I felt as though all the lights had been put out.

My parents had had to live through all this in their old age. Today they would be glad if they knew that the light of Dietrich's memory was kept alive; that he lives on in countless hundreds of men and women both old and young. His writings have been translated into many languages. Bonhoeffer student hostels and community hostels, schools, homes, streets and even churches in Germany, as well as one church in London, bear his name and bear witness to his memory. To many students he has become an inspiring example and from the pulpits his words go forth, those words which he put into practice in his life and in his death.

I had always hoped that the Allied troops had firm plans of their own for sending in paratroops to take possession of the concentration camps before the ground troops came too near to them, and for liberating their inmates. Many of the English had joined with us in believing that this would be the case—though perhaps in telling us this they were only trying to allay our anxieties. In any case it remained nothing more than a dream. Whether it really did belong to the realm of the impossible I am, it is true, unable to judge. But I could not rid myself of the suspicion that it was not done because the conduct of the war had become so embittered, a fact which is also illustrated by the disastrous policy towards the German opposition. The Bishop of Chichester had written to us that at the time Churchill was dedicated 'to fighting, to the exclusion of all else'.

As soon as the Bishop of Chichester was informed of the deaths of my brothers and brothers-in-law he wrote to us as follows:

The Palace, Chichester   22 July 1945

My dear friends,

I cannot express to you how sad I am for and with you both at Dietrich's death with Klaus. I had a cable in New York but did not know how to reach you immediately, and indeed believed that a letter posted in Chichester on my return would reach you as soon as anything I could write in U.S.A. Alas! Dietrich and Klaus had already been murdered when Visser't Hooft told us of the death sentence being impossible to carry out—at least so I suppose. For you, my dear Sabine, the agony of thus losing your dearest brother, so close to you, and Klaus with him, is sharp indeed. Nothing can fill the gap, though your husband and your daughters will become all the greater comfort. I feel for you both—and your whole family—with all my heart. And for the Church in Germany the loss is as heavy a loss as can be imagined. For Dietrich, had God willed, could have done so mighty a work in the long and troubled process of recovery and revival. But the work he has done for the Confessional Church and so both for Germany and for the Ecumenical Church is of a value beyond measure. He was unflinching and clear sighted and devoted in faith and loyalty to his Master. And he never thought of himself. He was a martyr for Christ—and for the Germany he loved and in which, in God's purpose for which, he so fully believed. I should like somewhere, in place and time most suitable to you, to have a service of remembrance for him—to thank God for this brave, steadfast and suffering soul, and to pray that the life he gave for others may be blessed and fruitful.

May God comfort you both, my dear friends—to whom Dietrich brought me—and to whom I shall always for his and your own sake cling. With my love and prayers, in which Mrs Bell unites.

Your affectionate

George Cicestr

In answer to my letter thanking him for all the support and help he had given us the Bishop replied:

The Palace, Chichester   25th July 1945

My dear Sabine,

(If I may thus call you.) I am deeply grateful for your letter. All you say, so undeserved, is a great comfort to me; and I am very happy to have Dietrich's photograph. You know something, I am sure, of what his friendship and love meant to me. My heart is full of sorrow for you, for alas, it is only too true that the gap he and Klaus leave can never be filled. I pray that God may give peace and strength to your parents, and to all who mourn, and bless them.

I am greatly looking forward to seeing you both on Friday. I do not know whether your daughters will be there; but my telegram just sent will of course include them.

I sent a brief tribute to *The Times*, with a note to the Editor, asking him to print it. There is a summary of it, without my name, and with certain parts omitted, in this morning's paper.*

* The following letter was sent by the Editor of *The Times* in reply to the Bishop: 'My Lord—The Editor has asked me to thank you for so kindly sending him an account of Pastor D. Bonhoeffer's part in the resistance to Hitler. Owing to the very great number of obituary notices and tributes awaiting publication he fears that it will not be possible to find space to print an account much of which has so recently appeared in the Press, but he has been able briefly to give the main facts including the date and place of the memorial service. A cutting of the paragraph is enclosed with the Editor's compliments'.

I thought you might like to have the full text.

Yours very sincerely,

George Cicestr

The Bishop of Chichester asked us whether we would think it right for the memorial service to be broadcast to Germany as well. We agreed and then journeyed to London together with the children.

The memorial service for Dietrich and Klaus was held by the Bishop of Chichester on the 27th July 1945 in the Church of the Holy Trinity, Brompton. Pastor Franz Hildebrandt and Dr Julius Rieger also spoke. The great congregation, composed of Germans and English together, rose and we sang the first hymn:

> *For all the saints who from their labours rest,*
> *Who thee by faith before the world confest,*
> *Thy name, O Jesu, be forever blest.*
> *Alleluya!*

All seven verses of this beautiful hymn were sung, and we have never forgotten them. Finally came the prayer of supplication and thanksgiving pronounced by the Bishop of Chichester. After this the hymn 'Hark a herald voice is calling' was sung in German and English. Then followed the sermon on Matthew 10:17-42. The choir of the community to which Dietrich had formerly ministered gave a particularly beautiful rendering of *Wer nur den lieben Gott lässt walten* (Who makes the will of God his only rule), and later we all sang together the hymn which Dietrich had arranged to be sung the last time he preached in London: *Mir nach, spricht Christus, unser Held* (Follow me, says Christ, our hero). This was followed by the Bishop's sermon. In this he said of Dietrich, amongst other things:

'He was quite clear in his convictions, and for all that he was so young and unassuming, he saw the truth and spoke it out with absolute freedom and without fear. When he came to me all unexpectedly in 1942 at Stockholm as the emissary of the Resistance to Hitler, he was, as always, absolutely open and quite untroubled about his own person, his safety. Wherever he went and whoever he spoke with—whether young or old—he was fearless, regardless of himself and, with it all, devoted heart and soul to his parents, his friends, his country as God willed it to be, to his Church and to his Master.'

In his sermon, the Bishop of Chichester also paid tribute to the memory of our brother Klaus and our brothers-in-law, Rüdiger Schleicher and Hans von Dohnanyi, whose fate had been revealed to us only at a later stage.

The Bishop ended with the words, 'The blood of martyrs is the seed of the Church'. The combined German-English congregation felt this to be a unique service and all were deeply moved by it.

We spent the evening with the Bishop in a quiet club, where we were joined by Kurt Hahn, the educationalist and headmaster of Gordonstoun which he had founded in 1934. As Director of 'Salem' Castle, the German boarding school which he had brought into being, he, too, had been driven out by the Nazis in 1933. One of the pupils who left 'Salem' with Kurt Hahn at that time to enter his newly-founded school of Gordonstoun had been Prince Philip, Duke of Edinburgh. Hahn, too, had known my brother Dietrich, and once more we spoke of the days when Dietrich and the Bishop had last met in Sweden. We also discussed how from the ruin and sacrifice of it all, strength, hope, and a right orientation for the future were to be won, how the true significance of all this might be made known to a new generation, and how we could help it to advance. The Bishop and Hahn told us of much 'good-will' but also of great bewilderment in many places, the more so since social upheavals of all kinds remained an ever-present possibility and could bring all plans to nothing.

In these first months after the war we were still unable to make any contact with our parents and surviving relatives. In March 1945 we had become acquainted with an English officer, with whose help a way was finally opened to us in August 1945 to write to my parents. Through him we also learned that my parents in Berlin had heard the broadcast of the memorial service from London, and that it was through this service that they had finally come to know with complete certainty that Dietrich was dead. My parents received incontestable news of the murder of Klaus and Rüdiger Schleicher at the end of May. The uncertainty as to the fate of Hans von Dohnanyi lasted the longest. The long martyrdom he had endured in the concentration camp at Sachsenhausen culminated in his execution at the same time at which Dietrich was murdered in the concentration camp at Flossenbürg.

Some days later the long-awaited first letter from my parents in Berlin arrived at Oxford. It was with a heavy heart that my mother had written her news to us. She had done so under great pressure of time, for it had been arranged that a returning English officer should take the letter with him, and he was only allowed to carry documents written in English in his luggage. Thus my mother had been forced to compress all the terrible events which had taken place into terse sentences. The letter ran as follows:

Berlin   23rd July 1945

My dearest children,

We have just been told that an opportunity has arisen for us to send you our greetings and news. It is now three years, I believe, since we received the last letters from you. Now we have just heard that Gert sent a telegram to Switzerland in order to obtain news of the fate of our dear Dietrich. From this we conclude that you are all still alive, and that is a great consolation for us in our deep sorrow over the fate of our dear Klaus, Dietrich and Rudiger.

Dietrich spent eighteen months in the military prison at Tegel. Last October he was handed over to the Gestapo and transferred to the S.S. prison in Prinz-Albrecht-Strasse. During the early days of February he was taken from there to various concentration camps such as Buchenwald and Flossenbürg near Weiden. We did not know where he was.

His fiancée, Maria von Wedemeyer, who was living with us at this time, attempted to find out for herself where he was. But in this she was unsuccessful. After the victory of the Allies we heard that Dietrich was still alive. But later we received news that he had been murdered by the Gestapo a little before the Americans arrived.

At Tegel Dietrich was still able to continue his academic work. Thus while he was in prison he wrote a large part of his

'Ethics'. He also wrote some beautiful poems. At Tegel we were able to go and visit him every week and bring him books and food. During these visits we very often spoke of you and your future. Dietrich was so hopeful of being able to see you again after the war.

Klaus and Rüdiger were arrested by the Gestapo in October for their part in the events of the 20th July. On the 2nd February they were condemned to death. Klaus was subjected to torture, but he and Rüdiger stood firm throughout.

Klaus wrote us a wonderful last letter and also one to his children. Ursel was able to see Rüdiger from time to time. He was very much loved by his fellow prisoners but he suffered terribly during the time that he was in prison. Shortly before the Russians arrived Klaus and Rüdiger were shot by the Gestapo.

Ursel is now living with us together with the children, because on the 27th April, in the very last days of the war, they were bombed out. Hans-Walter was taken prisoner by the Americans but has now been released and is helping on a farm.

Klaus' children were evacuated to Holstein. Emmi stayed here so as to be able to visit Klaus. Now she has gone to her children. Her house, too, was completely destroyed by the bombing. Hans (von Dohnanyi) was arrested with Dietrich and on the same day. In prison he caught diphtheria and it left him with a permanent disability. Later he was transferred to the concentration camp at Sachsenhausen. There most of the prisoners were killed before the Russians arrived. We do not yet know whether Hans is still alive.

Hans and Christel's house at Sakrow has been taken over by the Russians. So she is living with Christoph and Bärbel at Dahlem. Klaus Dohnanyi had to join the Labour Service. He is now working on a farm belonging to relatives of Maria von Wedemeyer in Bavaria.

During the fighting around Leipzig, Karl-Friedrich was with his family at Friedrichsbrunn. His institute is completely destroyed by bombs. Susi, too, has been completely bombed out.

Walter Dress is a pastor at Dahlem and is once more giving lectures. Eberhard (Bethge), the husband of Renate, was also in the Gestapo prison in the Lehrter Strasse. But he was liberated when the Russians took Berlin.

191

The Bonhoeffers

Aunt Elizabeth lost her life during a heavy air attack on the railway station at Dresden.

From all this news you can imagine what we parents have been suffering all this time in our old age. And now there is not enough food for everyone. Greatly though we long to see you again we cannot advise you to return to us here. We have no news from Göttingen. Here it is, of course, quite impossible either to write or to telephone. We are sorry not to have your last address but hope that this letter will reach you. All our love goes out to you and we hope to see you again in better times.

It would give us great joy if you could send us some news of yourselves and the children by the same channel as this reaches you.

Your Mother and Father

In 1945 reports appeared in the English Press of the dead, starving and pitifully tortured human beings whom the Americans and English had discovered in the Nazi concentration camps. After this the attitude towards the Germans in England became unmistakably more hostile. The English, otherwise so patient and moderate, were filled with indignation, and the people were aroused. In the buses the Nazi atrocities were discussed by young and old alike. The disgust was genuine and universal. It was a great disgrace to be Germans. It was painful to be spoken to about one's German nationality. In fact we refugees had long since been deprived of this by a Nazi law, but who was so well-informed as to know this? Well-meaning strangers among the English in offices or hotels now merely used to ask, 'You are Swiss, aren't you?' or 'You are Norwegian, aren't you?' No one wanted to suggest that we were Germans.

Once when Gert and I were waiting in a queue of about twenty-five people at a bus stop on our usual route home we happened to meet a friend of Gert's student days who was living in Oxford and Gert exchanged a few words of German with him. At this a man in the queue shouted at Gert, 'So you are a German. What are you doing here in England? Go to your own country where your concentration camps are! All Germans belong in there!'

I replied, 'You don't in the least know whom you are talking to. We have just lost two brothers and two brothers-in-law in concentration camps at the hands of the Gestapo. We are victims of Nazi oppression. Here it is printed on our identification papers.'

But he neither saw nor believed anything that I said and continued to insist that he did not want there to be any more Germans in his country. And with an eye to the bystanders, seeking to gain their agreement, he called out 'Once a German ever a German!'

But the other people remained silent. One lady shook her head as she said to us, 'He is a ruffian.'

About this time our daughter Marianne was an undergraduate of seventeen and together with two other refugee girls she went on a hiking expedition. On a dusty country road a car stopped and a gentleman offered to give the girls a lift to the next youth hostel. They gladly got in and he began a conversation, asking the two Oxford undergraduates to tell him about themselves. Then suddenly he turned to the eldest and asked, 'Where do you come from?' This was the well-known and much-dreaded question to which the reply given by many refugees was simply 'Switzerland'. But Hilde answered in all honesty, 'Berlin'. At this the Englishman straightaway jammed on his brakes, opened the door and turned the girls out, though it was he who had offered them a ride, with a furious 'Get out at once! I will not have any Germans in my car.' The three girls returned from their expedition much depressed.

On the 6th August 1945 the first atomic bomb fell on Hiroshima, four years after the Japanese attack on the American fleet at Pearl Harbour. At the time we were in Cheltenham at a conference of a Christian youth organization at which Gert was giving a lecture. The number of the Japanese who were killed had been disclosed, and all the young people at the conference were utterly shocked and strongly condemned the use of the uranium atom bomb. At that time Professor Otto Hahn, together with other German atomic physicists, was being held captive in England. According to Professor Heisenberg, when he received news of what had taken place Hahn was so deeply shocked and reduced to despair that it was feared that he would attempt to take his own life. On the 15th, VJ Day, the victory over Japan was celebrated in America and England. The relief felt in England was quite unmistakable. Our English acquaintances had been very anxious about their prisoners of war in Japanese hands. One year after the war we came to know Michael Foester, a don at Christchurch. The first day on which we had occasion to speak of Dietrich he took out of his wallet a copy of the poem, 'Who Am I?', the translation of Dietrich's *Wer bin ich?* The English version is as follows:

> *Who am I? they often tell me*
> *I stepped from my cell's confinement*
> *Calmly, cheerfully, firmly,*
> *Like a squire from his country house.*
> *Who am I? They often tell me*
> *I used to speak to my warders*
> *Freely and friendly and clearly,*
> *As though they were mine to command.*
> *Who am I? They also tell me*
> *I bore the days of misfortune*
> *Equably, smilingly, proudly*
> *Like one accustomed to win.*
>
> *Am I then really all that which other men tell of?*
> *Or am I only what I myself know of myself?*
> *Restless and longing and sick, like a bird in a cage,*
> *Struggling for breath, as though hands were*
> *compressing my throat,*
> *Yearning for colours, for flowers, for the voices of birds,*
> *Thirsting for words of kindness, for neighbourliness,*
> *Tossing in expectation of great events,*
> *Powerlessly trembling for friends at an infinite distance,*
> *Weary and empty at praying, at thinking, at making,*
> *Faint, and ready to say farewell to it all?*
>
> *Who am I? This or the other?*
> *Am I one person today and tomorrow another?*
> *Am I both at once? A hypocrite before others,*
> *And before myself a contemptibly woebegone weakling?*
> *Or is something within me still like a beaten army,*
> *Fleeing in disorder from victory already achieved?*
>
> *Who am I? They mock me these lonely questions of mine.*
> *Whoever I am, Thou knowest O God, I am thine!*

Michael Foster told us that he had been carrying these verses about with him wherever he went, and that he could find no words to express how much this poem meant to him. Later, in 1947, Michael Foster went to Cologne as a professor of political science and by his openness, kindness and his sympathy won the hearts of many German students. After two years he returned once more to his Oxford College.

A great part of the years 1945-47 were occupied with packing up parcels. To me it was a great consolation to be able to send something regularly to my parents and family, and above all that we could once more write to each other. This was made possible for me through English friends in official positions in Berlin. The parcels to my parents were faithfully delivered.

On the 3rd August we received the following letter from Karl-Friedrich about everything which had taken place:

August 3rd

Dear Sabine and dear Gert,

I have just been having a week's stay here in Berlin with our parents and sisters. Soon, however, I shall have to leave for Leipzig, and there I shall be under Russian control.

With regard to the fate of Hans [von Dohnanyi] we have no absolute proof as yet, but really I cannot see any possible alternative. He had been very active for many years and was one of the leading figures in the secret resistance movement against Hitler. He was in contact with almost everybody who was prepared to work with the resistance. This is not the place to go into details. From the beginning of the war Dietrich worked with him in the resistance. You cannot imagine how much courage, prudence, caution and endurance was necessary, how often we all expected the imminent breakdown of this criminal tyranny (I have since heard that no less than five attempts were made on Hitler's life), or how often we were disappointed. Our parents were aware of what they were doing, approved of it and gave them assistance. I believe there can have been very few families in Germany during the past twelve years in which there was such complete agreement on political matters, and there is no doubt that this spirit gave them strength to continue their plans. Although Rüdiger did not play any active part in the conspiracy, he did know of it. You know that he was a man who was incapable of lying and it was this that led to his death. At the time when Klaus [Bonhoeffer] was arrested there was little hope that he could be saved. But later he and Rüdiger became quite hopeful in view of the fact that we had succeeded in postponing the carrying out of the sentence. The treatment of Dietrich [Bonhoeffer] and Hans [von Dohnanyi] was very decent so long as they were prisoners of the military court. We were able to visit them every week and send them food and books. In the autumn of 1944 Dietrich was transferred to a prison of the S.S. and after that it became almost impossible to contact him. Some weeks ago I met Goerdeler's son who had seen him in the middle of April. Dietrich told him that at least he had enough to eat and Goerdeler thought that he looked quite well and not too thin. Klaus was cruelly tortured. Later, after his sentence his treatment improved a little. Most of the warders at least were not bad people and they did give him the food we sent him. He had permission to read but was generally kept in chains as also was Rüdiger. Hans got diphtheria in prison followed by a paralysis affecting his whole body but especially his legs. This delayed his trial and that of Dietrich. At the moment we still do not know whether they were even sentenced or whether they were simply murdered out of hand. But really it makes no difference.

Of course you are anxious to know how our parents are. Their mental constancy and firmness are astonishing. But their physical strength has diminished rather rapidly during the past years and still more during the past weeks. We hope that before too much time has passed you will be granted a permit and be able to come and see us. There is nothing that would give them so much joy.

With all our love,
Yours ever,

Karl-Friedrich

In December 1946 while we were still waiting for it to become possible for us to travel to Germany, Eberhard Bethge succeeded in coming to Oxford to visit us. He at least could give us a first-hand account of what had happened. His time of captivity and the pain that Dietrich's death had given him had marked him deeply. In the meantime he had married Renate Schleicher, and they had christened their son Dietrich.

At the invitation of some of his scientist colleagues my brother Karl-Friedrich made the journey to England and came to see us. This was a great joy, even though our reunion was clouded with infinite pain. He had become very haggard, and as he looked at me he had my mother's eyes. Of course we had much news to exchange. Unfortunately the time we could spend together was far too brief. Not long afterwards Dean Grüber, too, came over and visited us in Oxford. It was known in England how much good he had done for those who had been persecuted under the Nazi régime. One day Theodor Heuss, at that time an active member of the Parliamentary Assembly, came to see us. He was a friend of my brother Klaus and his wife, and wanted to give us some news of our family and of his work. We were glad of every visitor from Germany who was able to get through the barriers. Heuss looked very thin, pale and careworn, but he seemed to feel that England was doing him good. I will never forget these days that we spent with visitors from Germany, with all that we now heard from them by direct word of mouth.

In 1946 my husband was asked by the Foreign Office whether he was willing to hold political lectures in the German prisoner-of-war camps and whether he would be prepared to undertake courses of such lectures at Beaconsfield. He would be fetched by car and driven to the various different camps which were scattered about the country. This work gave him joy because the lectures were listened to very attentively and discussed very fully by the prisoners of war. Generally he lectured on two successive days, spent the night at the camp where he was lecturing, and at the same time became acquainted with the English officers.

On one occasion Gert had to go to the camp for senior general officers at Bridgend, where at that time Brauchitsch, Manstein, Kleist, Sänger-Etterlin, Blumentritt, Rundstedt and other officers were being held. Even in the prison camps the hierarchy was still strictly observed. Once the Field Marshals had spoken in the discussion, no other officer would speak after them. During his captivity Brauchitsch occupied himself with writing the preliminary draft of a new German constitution. He had written it in a school exercise book and drawn a large Iron Cross on the cover. After he had completed it he handed it to my husband. On this visit Gert spoke about the 20th July 1944. Rundstedt did not come to this lecture, but afterwards he sought out Gert and they came to speak of the offensive in the Ardennes. Gert asked why the Ardennes offensive had still been persisted with in view of the hopelessness of the position and the many victims it claimed. Had the Germans' judgement of the situation perhaps been different from this? 'No,' replied Rundstedt, it had been quite clear to him that the position was indeed hopeless.

'Then why did you not refuse to undertake the offensive?' asked my husband.

Rundstedt's answer was, 'Because if I had I would have been shot.'

On the 1st October 1945 my husband received a letter from a Squadron-Leader Falconer which I reproduce here:

1st October 1945

H. M. Falconer, S/Ldr

Dear Professor,

I knew your wife's twin brother, Dietrich Bonhoeffer, very well. I first met him on the 24th February this year when I arrived in Buchenwald from Sachsenhausen. Although we were still nominally in solitary confinement we were able to frighten our two guards into closing their eyes to a certain amount of contact.

Furthermore, at this time your brother-in-law was sharing a cell with General von Rabenau, the Prussian writer of military history. I think they were the only pair of prisoners sharing a cell who got on really well together and enjoyed each other's company. On the 2nd April this year we were both rushed away from Buchenwald because of the American advance across the River Fulda. After one night in the civil prison in Regensburg we were taken to Schönberg in the Bavarian Forest where we all lived together in a room which was originally the girls' infirmary. On Sunday your brother-in-law held a short service which moved us all, Catholics and Protestants alike, by its simple sincerity. Your brother-in-law was very happy during the whole of the time I knew him, and did a great deal to keep some of the weaker brethren from depression and anxiety.

He spent a good deal of time with Wasily Wasiliew Kokorin, Molotov's nephew, who was a delightful young man although an atheist. I think your brother-in-law divided his time with him between instilling the foundations of Christianity and learning Russian. Your brother-in-law was taken away from us, together with General von Rabenau, and sent to Flossenbürg where, as you already know, they were both murdered by the S.S. at the order of the Gestapo. Later in Dachau I met an old friend of mine who had been in the cells in Flossenbürg. He had been in touch with Dietrich and the General, and he told me that, to within a very short time of their death, neither had any idea of what was to happen to them.

A Dane* who saw the two shot, through a hole in the wooden screen of his cell window, told me that they both died with a calmness and dignity which made him realise that all Germans are not of the stamp of the Gestapo.

I am afraid that this is all I can tell you about Dietrich, but at least you have the consolation of knowing that he was spared the agonies of anticipation and died in peace.

Yours sincerely,

H. M. Falconer, S/Ldr

Two years more passed before we could be reunited with my parents and family. We could not obtain any permit to travel, although we moved heaven and earth, and the Bishop of Chichester, too, spared no pains to help us on our way.

After all we had heard about circumstances in Germany we could not contemplate a definitive return without first having seen Germany once more for ourselves, especially on account of our daughters. Marianne had begun to read for her degree at Oxford and in the meantime they had come to think of Oxford as their home. Many young Germans were at that time struggling to leave Germany. But only a few were successful in getting abroad for the first time. In 1947, after endless efforts, the British authorities finally gave us the necessary permit to travel to Germany.

In England the attitude towards the German refugees was divided. Many English people pressed for the return of the refugees. Most, however, understood the position of those who, after all that had befallen Jews and opponents of the Nazi régime

---

* It is not known if the Dane actually watched these executions or those of two other men, or if he wrote this in order to comfort the family.

(and were there any among the refugees who had not lost some of those belonging to them in the concentration camps?), wanted to test conditions in Germany for themselves. Many English people actually considered that to return to Germany constituted a weakness of character and a breach of faith with the country which had given them refuge. In America, those who had emigrated in 1933 had been able to become American citizens even before the outbreak of war. In England one could only obtain British citizenship after five years, and during the war not at all. Yet here there were many 'non-Aryans' who had only decided to escape as a result of the pogroms of the year 1938. These were still German despite the fact that under the Nazi laws of deprivation of German nationality they had become stateless soon after their flight abroad. In those days none of our friends had yet returned to Germany. Our reason for wanting to travel to Germany was above all to see our parents, sisters and brother again.

Finally, in the early summer of 1947, we reached a point at which this became possible, but we had to leave our daughters behind. They were not allowed to travel. The departure was swift. The crossing was calm, the weather hazy, but finally we saw land. The Belgian coast suddenly rose up and lay in the sun before us. Our hearts began to beat. For eight whole years we had not set foot upon the Continent and had been complete island dwellers. A great excitement gripped us. The Belgian porters rushed shouting onto the ship and almost tore our luggage from us. What verve! What speed! And how much smaller these Belgian men were! The boat train was already waiting and soon we were sitting in it bound for Brussels. By midnight we were exhausted with looking out of the window. When the train drew very slowly into the ruined and burnt out station of Aachen there was deep quiet. The first German signboards appeared, and now the first words spoken in German upon German soil: 'Karl, where have you put the lamp?'

And these few little words were enough to make one's heart stand still. 'So this is how you have been speaking all these years', I thought to myself.

No one got in; no one got out. Dark night, rain, ruins, solitude, quiet—only the hammering of the man who had been trying to find the lamp.

Index

Index